Caleb S. Henry

Doctor Oldham at Greystones, and his talk there

Caleb S. Henry

Doctor Oldham at Greystones, and his talk there

ISBN/EAN: 9783743367845

Manufactured in Europe, USA, Canada, Australia, Japa

Cover: Foto ©ninafisch / pixelio.de

Manufactured and distributed by brebook publishing software (www.brebook.com)

Caleb S. Henry

Doctor Oldham at Greystones, and his talk there

GREYSTONES, ENTRANCE FRONT.

DOCTOR OLDHAM

AT GREYSTONES,

AND

HIS TALK THERE.

De omnibus rebus et quibusdam aliis.

NEW YORK:
D. APPLETON AND COMPANY,
346 & 348 BROADWAY.
LONDON: 16 LITTLE BRITAIN.
1860.

ENTERED, according to Act of Congress, in the year 1859, by
D. APPLETON & CO.,
In the Clerk's Office of the District Court of the United States for the Southern District of New York.

CONTENTS.

CHAPTER I.

The library table and Mrs. Oldham's opinion of it—Idea-images; the caution necessary in reducing them to feet and inches—Drawers made to prevent husband and wife pulling together; yet serving to a more loving harmony—Shattered ideals—How Mrs. Oldham was like Sir Isaac Newton's dog, and Doctor Oldham not like Sir Isaac—The wisdom of nonsense, ... 1

CHAPTER II.

Which grows out of the inartistic way this book began; but gives the author a chance to speak of the courteous reader of the last age; and also to explain himself to the courteous reader of the present day, . . 13

CHAPTER III.

Which comes between the last chapter and the next one—The reader may omit if he will; but he will lose something if he does, ... 20

CONTENTS.

PAGE

CHAPTER IV.

The library not made for the table—The recess that was not realized and the window that was—The library as finished—Doctor Oldham's opinion about good company—He quotes Doctor Southey and discourses about him, ... 27

CHAPTER V.

Greystones: and what Downing might have said if he had had the altering of the plan of it, ... 38

CHAPTER VI.

Henry Reed—Coleridge on Wordsworth s verses—The Doctor's theory of the distinction between man and the brutes, and also of the edible and potable universe, as propounded to Professor Clare, ... 49

CHAPTER VII.

Short, if not sweet—Difference between the author and Rabelais, and some other celebrated writers, ... 62

CHAPTER VIII.

The Doctor visits Mrs. Rossville's school—And tells his wife what he said to the little folks there—Mr. Grim—How God takes care the children shall not be hurt by bad catechisms, ... 66

CHAPTER IX.

More talk about children—The good Lord's contrivances to prevent their being shut out of the world of fiction, ... 76

CHAPTER X.

Glimpses biographical and auto-biographical—With observations interspersed that are worth a chapter in themselves, ... 84

CONTENTS.

CHAPTER XI.

How nature shows her gladness—June and Junefulness—When a nose is a good thing—Is it an organ for the beautiful—The glories of October—Nature's picture gallery—Art and its limitations—Mrs. Oldham asks two very great questions, ... 93

CHAPTER XII.

Professor Clare—The Doctor's talk about the starry heavens—Addison and Shakspeare—Word-painting and other painting—Where the universe ends and how it is filled—Mrs. Oldham's two questions are not answered, ... 104

CHAPTER XIII.

More about the stars and the earth—Pantheism—Whether any thing can become so small as to become nothing and yet remain something—Time and space—Mrs. Oldham's two great questions again, and the way they were answered, ... 117

CHAPTER XIV.

The Doctor preaches to his daughter—Quotes Wordsworth and gets into heroics—Also he fulfils a scriptural duty—Remarkable street-sweepers and knife-grinders—Comforting doctrine concerning shirt-making and stocking mending, ... 133

CHAPTER XV.

Wherein the Doctor says pshaw to something advanced by the author, and advances his own notions—Comfort and swill not the highest felicity for rational beings—The world needs martyrs, but Crooke Racket not the right type, ... 150

CHAPTER XVI.

Lot's house in Sodom—Jonah in New York—The Doctor villifies universal suffrage and an elective judiciary in a very shocking way; and makes the most unsupposable suppositions—An extraordinary ticket for city offices, ... 158

CHAPTER XVII.

A short chapter on judge-making—Not amusing; and not so likely to be interesting to those who need, as to those who do not need, the instruction it contains, ... 176

CHAPTER XVIII.

Something on universal suffrage and sacred rights—Wherein is seen how Professor Claro and Pelham Brief differ from each other, and the Doctor from them both, ... 183

CHAPTER XIX.

Hard and dry, perhaps—But going to the bottom of a subject immensely important to be understood in this country, ... 193

CHAPTER XX.

Very short, perhaps unpalatable—Yet, if true, ought not to give offence to any good man, ... 209

CHAPTER XXI.

Also short—Not without interest for some minds—But likely to displease two sorts of readers and to shock one of them, ... 213

CHAPTER XXII.

The Doctor at a woman's rights convention—What he did not say there, but would have said if he had said any thing, ... 220

CHAPTER XXIII.

On Dee-deeing, ... 247

CONTENTS.

CHAPTER XXIV.
Tweedledum and Tweedledee, ... 254

CHAPTER XXV.
Some of the Doctor's notions about conversation—His practice is another question, ... 258

CHAPTER XXVI.
Preliminary to another, ... 263

CHAPTER XXVII.
Of owls, ... 265

CHAPTER XXVIII.
The Doctor says some things that sound very strange to Mrs. Garland—Bad Christians and good heathen—Mr. Grim—The necessity for a good God, ... 266

CHAPTER XXIX.
Professor Clare gets back to Japan, and the Doctor is unduly severe upon cant and the gospel of cotton fields, ... 278

CHAPTER XXX.
Mr. Stockjob Pile—Alderman Gubbins—Hardhead Bullion—Bob Slender—It takes something inside to make something—which is declared at the end of the chapter, ... 285

CHAPTER XXXI.
About Caspar Tuberose and his wife—With other things touching the constitution of a gentleman, ... 297

CHAPTER XXXII.
The Doctor's horse—What and why about him, ... 318

CHAPTER XXXIII.

All-hang-together-ness, ... 321

CHAPTER XXXIV.

L'Envoy, perhaps—Containing something natural—And also something supernatural from which nothing came except some natural remarks of the Doctor's, ... 332

DOCTOR OLDHAM.

CHAPTER I.

THE LIBRARY TABLE AND MRS. OLDHAM'S OPINION OF IT.—IDEA-IMAGES; THE CAUTION NECESSARY IN REDUCING THEM TO FEET AND INCHES.—DRAWERS MADE TO PREVENT HUSBAND AND WIFE PULLING TOGETHER; YET SERVING TO A MORE LOVING HARMONY.—SHATTERED IDEALS.—HOW MRS. OLDHAM WAS LIKE SIR ISAAC NEWTON'S DOG AND DOCTOR OLDHAM NOT LIKE SIR ISAAC. —THE WISDOM OF NONSENSE.

THE family were all gathered around the large library table, as usual of an evening. I said the large library table; Mrs. Oldham thought it too large, and besides she disliked the shape of it. It was a square-cornered oblong table, and she would have preferred it to be oval. The Doctor, I know, secretly agreed with her; at least he came to be of the same way of thinking after she had expressed her opinion—a thing he was very apt to do. But he had not frankly confessed his whole mind to her about it; he had only told her that the oval shape might perhaps have looked better, without much diminishing the size of it, which he had all along insisted was no larger than it ought to be to give room for them all to sit around it—a point he had set his heart on from the beginning.

The truth was, Mrs. Oldham, with her homely, honest way of speaking out her mind, had hurt the Doctor's feelings, without knowing it or intending it. But she had hurt them weeks before, the very first time she saw the table. And this was the way of it.

The Doctor had set his heart on having a Library table, truly and properly such, a table for a library, one to hold books, one that would allow a good many books to lie on it, and large enough for all the family to sit around it, and read and write without interfering with each other, with room besides for any friend that might chance to drop in upon them. Such was his ideal of a library table. He had long indulged his mind's eye with the pleasing image. It had grown, in fact, to be a weakness of his, something that he in a sort doted on realizing some day. So he had gone and bespoken it six months before the library was finished and ready to receive it, before indeed the foundations of the newly-built part of Greystones were laid. He had ordered it to be made six feet long and three feet wide, going only by the image in his mind's eye, and guessing even at the dimensions of that without having ever measured and noted any actual table of such a width and length. He had done so too without consulting Mrs. Oldham, which was something very unusual with him; for he had a high opinion of her good sense. Indeed he was wont to say, that in point of practical wisdom he thought his wife very much his superior; but in the faculty of seeing through a speculative millstone without any hole in it, he did not scruple to say he did not consider her so highly gifted as Jeremy Bentham or himself. This matter of the library table was undoubtedly a practical affair, the getting it made at least, and yet, owing, he supposed, to the pre-occupation of his mind with his ideal, he had neglected to secure her advice and sanction, I mean as to its exact form and dimensions—for he had told her, in a general and passing way, that he was going to have a library table made—but as she made no particular inquiries, not imagining it was to be ordered so long beforehand, it happened that nothing more was said.

So the table was made and brought home and set in its place. Mrs. Oldham looked at it for a moment or two, and then said:

"Husband, I don't like it. It is too large, and the shape of it doesn't please me. Altogether, it looks like a table for a bank parlor or for an insurance office."

Dear woman! She little thought how inwardly aghast her words struck the Doctor. In the placid sincerity of her womanly and wifely heart, there was the most perfect, and at the same time perfectly unreflected and unconscious confidence in the impossibility of her saying anything, or of his taking anything she could say, in any other than a kindly spirit. So she had spoken as she felt, without thinking of it even as a matter in which there might be a difference of taste between them, still less dreaming that she was giving him pain. She knew nothing of his visions and his images. She did not know this table was his realized ideal. She knew nothing of all he had been dreaming about so long, and which of late, as the time of fulfilment drew near, had so filled his mind's eye. He had never told her; although he is one of the most open-hearted persons I ever knew, and communicative to a fault, as his wife often told him, and as he himself has had too many occasions to be conscious of, when he has, in his frank, confiding way, laid himself open to the stupid, the brutal, or the malicious. Yet he had never told anybody, not even her. You may think this strange, but I do not. On the contrary, I think it altogether natural; for always in your dreaming, speculative natures, like the Doctor's, there are some cherished fancies which, with all their frankness and unreserve, they are shy of revealing to any human creature—from a half consciousness of their weakness about them and their inability to bear any exposure of it to the unsympathetic, and yet an instinctive sense of the impossibility of anybody but themselves fully sympathizing with them. You may think this an over deep and wise lesson in human nature to bring in here to explain such a trifling thing as the Doctor's not telling his wife his secret fancies about a table. But it is a true lesson, and one that everybody ought to learn; one that will explain a great many other things besides the Doctor's silence; and you ought to be thankful for a lesson of wisdom, however trivial the occasion that leads me to give it to you.

But so it was, the Doctor had never told even his wife,—not, of course, from any deliberate purpose of concealment, but unconsciously, from the influence of the feeling I have mentioned ; and so she could not know what she was trampling upon. She would not have hurt his feelings for the world. But she had. She had demolished his ideal ; she had shattered his vision. He could not stand up against her opinion. He never could in such matters. He had never been able all the time they had lived together to think right well of anything that did not suit her taste.

But now the shock was great. He could not bring himself to show how much he was wounded. He tried to hold up. He even defended his vilified ideal.

"Too large, my dear ? Why, it is only large enough for us all to sit about it of an evening in that comfortable pleasant way, which I am sure you think so nice. Besides, see here !" turning her attention away from the size of the table, "here are six drawers, one for each of us, three on one side and three on the other. This one is for me ; that opposite is yours; here is Phil's ; there Fred's ; this is Lilly's ; and this is for Cousin Kitty when she comes. It is so pleasant to have one's own drawer to put one's things into which one does not wish to leave lying on the table, and yet wants to have always near at hand."

"I see," said she, taking hold of her drawer and pulling it out, "but, husband, your six drawers are only three, each of them running through the whole width of the table and drawing out on either side. See, your drawer and mine are only one drawer with a partition across the middle and knobs on both ends; so, when you open your drawer on your side of the table, you draw mine after it out of my reach. What shall we do if we both wish to use our drawers at the same time?"

"Do?" said the Doctor, disconcerted at this new discovery to the discredit of his ideal, "do? do? Well, my dear," pinching his nose between the thumb and forefinger of his left hand, his usual resource in such cases, "I do not know that I can tell you what we must do. But I can tell you what we must not do. We must not do what you and I have always done hitherto."

"What do you mean?" she inquired.

"Pull together, my dear. We have always pulled together. But it will not do for us to pull our drawers together. We must pull them in the spirit of compromise, in the spirit of mutual compromise, my dear Mrs. Oldham, and then this very peculiarity in the make of our drawers,—a peculiarity for which I confess I do not see any good mechanical reason—will become, I will not say a memento to the practice of a virtue which even prudence, in a case like this, would dictate to merely selfish natures, but will become—as all outward things, however trivial, do become to right loving hearts — a sermon and a sacrament of divinest charity."

The Doctor paused, inwardly elated with the gentle excitement of his small sermon. The justice of his wife's objection was palpable, and there was not a single compensating advantage. But he did not like to own that the drawers were made in this absurd way by his own special direction, from a notion they would be handier—a notion he had got, not from ever actually seeing and handling any real drawers made in this fashion, but solely from contemplating the idea-image in his mind's eye.

He was glad to get off from the subject. But the truth is that, from this time,

> . . . . . The glory and the gleam,
> The consecration and the poet's dream,

began to fade from his realized ideal. He began to see his table through his wife's eyes. At length every time he looked at the long square-cornered thing, with its shining bronze imitation leather top, he saw it was not the thing he ought to have ordered. It was too large for the room, though he was still sure it was not too large for them all to sit at together; still, as a matter of proportion and good looks, it was too large; its shape was bad; and it looked too much like a "bank table"—he could not but confess it to himself, although he had felt that to be the unkindest cut in his wife's speech. He could not but secretly think how much better a nicely proportioned oval table, with a rich cloth cover of suitable color, would look.

But he had never brought himself to acknowledge it to her in a full, frank way, before this evening; because it was only this evening that he had got fairly over the chagrin and soreness of having the glory so torn from the vision of his long dreams. But to night he felt no difficulty in making the admission.

"Mrs. Oldham, my dear," said he, as they were drawing up to the table, "you were right. This is not the table we should have had. It is too large. It is not the right shape. It does look too much like a bank table."

"Husband," said she, in her kind placid voice—there was no triumph, no gratified vanity in her tone or look, any more than in her honest heart—"husband, you had better have consulted me before getting it made."

"I am sure of it, my dear," answered the Doctor, "you are an oracle of practical wisdom, Mrs. Oldham; I never neglect to obtain your advice and sanction in any matter of affairs, without finding reason to regret it in the end. But my forethoughts, you know, are very much like the Irishman's: they come afterwards. I am as full of notions as a Yankee, and as eager and incautious in realizing them as an Irishman, or, as my friend Idleman calls me, a very 'sanguinary man.' I have done many hasty things in my life that I repented of when they were past help. But there is one thing I have never repented of."

"What is that, husband?"

"Offering myself to you, Mrs. Oldham. You have been my good angel, my dear."

Mrs. Oldham's cheeks—still ruddy and round, though nearly a score of years had passed away since the event to which the Doctor referred—her matronly cheeks flushed slightly at this speech of her husband's; the more perhaps that not only the children and cousin Kitty were present, but also Maggie Crampton, who had come up from town on a visit, and was sitting at the moment between the Doctor and her.

He went on, however:

"But, in regard to this table, you do not know what a shock you inflicted upon me. I have reason to say to you, as the great Sir Isaac Newton said to his dog Diamond, 'O Diamond, Diamond, thou little knowest what harm thou hast done me!'"

"Bless me, husband, what have I done?"

"Shattered my ideal."

"Shattered your what?"

"My ideal, the vision of my mind. It is all in fragments. And the mischief you have done me, my dear, is not like that which Diamond did his master. That great philosopher could collect the scattered fragments and reproduce what Diamond had destroyed. But my ideal is irretrievable—it is shattered and lost forever."

"My dear husband," said she, in a pitying tone, "I am so sorry for your shattered ideal. But we will have a new and more beautiful one by and by. But indeed I do believe," she added, seeing the smallest trace of a twinkle in the Doctor's eye, "you are not sorry at all that you got so ugly a table made, seeing it has given you a chance to talk so much nonsense."

"Nonsense, my dear," said he, "I hope you think it charming nonsense. I trust you have a proper esteem for nonsense. It has in it the soul of the deepest wisdom. Like the motley of the Middle Ages, it often covers up more wit and sense than the knight's helmet, the earl's cap of maintenance, or the abbot's mitre. I declare to you some of the most solemn wise things I ever read have not seldom seemed to me the most painfully foolish or the most ridiculously absurd things in the world, while on the other hand, many things that Mrs. Slender thought very foolish, Miss Prim quite improper, and Doctor Rigid highly irreverent, have been to me the most charming lessons of virtue and religion, the purest goodness and the holiest worship, as full of pathos as of fun, making me laugh and making me cry, and making me better by both operations, filling my heart with more love to God and man than a dozen of Doctor Selah Solemn's Sermons on Sanctity, or Mrs. Softly's Serious Thoughts."

"What would become of us, my dear," he continued, "if all the books that Mrs. Slender thinks foolish, Miss Prim improper, and Doctor Rigid irreverent, were banished from the world;—no more Mother Goose's Melodies, nor the tragical fate of

Cock Robin, nor the immoral exploits of Puss in Boots, nor the mournful tale of Little Bopeep's Sheep's Tails, nor the story of the Three Bears with their three porridge pots and chairs and beds, and the mysterious old woman that got in at their door and out at their bedroom window, and has never been heard of since,—no more these and a thousand other nonsensical stories of foolish impossibilities for the little people to laugh over, and weep over, and wonder over; and no more Rabelais with his Pantagruel and Panurge, Cervantes with his Knight and Squire, Shakespeare with his more talkers of wise nonsense than I can name here; no more Uncle Toby and Corporal Trim; no more Doctor Primrose and Moses, nor Elia, nor Doctor Dove, nor Diedrick Knickerbocker, nor Mr. Sparrowgrass, for the delight of old folks and young folks both;—but all these, and hundreds of others, great like these in nonsense, done away with from the face of the earth, gone from human memory, and nothing left for the young people but Mrs. Sweet's Infant Hymns, and Professor Savethought's Great Things made Small, and nothing for the older folks but Dr. Solemn's Sermons and Mrs. Softly's Serious Thoughts! Think of it, my dear Mrs. Oldham! I really do not believe it would be good for the world."

The Doctor paused, quite affected by the picture he had drawn.

"But, husband," said Mrs. Oldham, "it is not every one that can see the soul of wisdom and goodness in those books of nonsense as well as you can, and therefore we ought to be glad there are such writings as Doctor Solemn's Sermons and Mrs. Softly's Serious Thoughts."

"True, my dear, true," replied the Doctor, "but let us also honor wise and holy nonsense."

CHAPTER II.

WHICH GROWS OUT OF THE INARTISTIC WAY THIS BOOK BEGAN; BUT GIVES THE AUTHOR A CHANCE TO SPEAK OF THE COURTEOUS READER OF THE LAST AGE; AND ALSO TO EXPLAIN HIMSELF TO THE COURTEOUS READER OF THE PRESENT DAY.

WHAT a fine old personage was the "Courteous Reader" for whom the writers of the seventeenth and eighteenth centuries wrote their books. How delightful the image or EIDOLON of him that rises before the mind's eye, as we notice in the writings of that time the thousand little tokens of thorough good understanding and mutual respect between the author and his reader. The picture is as distinct and agreeable as that of Sir Roger de Coverley; and we feel a positive regard for him such as we cannot help feeling for the good old Knight—who was himself undoubtedly one of the most courteous of the courteous readers of his day.

I trust the generation of them is not extinct,

although I do not so often perceive them to be expressly addressed in the books of our day: but this, I would fain believe, is owing only to that same change in the fashion and manner of the times which makes the polite forms of social intercourse to be so much more brief and simple, and causes so much to be now tacitly taken for granted in the way of courteous and kindly feeling which it was the custom to give ample and ceremonious expression to in those days.

So I am apt to think. Why not? Does anybody imagine Sir Roger de Coverley to be dead? I for one will never believe it. You will not indeed find him in the same fashion of dress, nor journeying along the road in the same way, nor with the same accidents of position and circumstance; but putting out of view the different way in which modern tailors make up men, and the different modes of travelling—all the accidents of the case, I am bold to say that every body has met him more than once on the steamboats and in the railway cars; some perhaps without knowing him, but some of us know him well—have been out in fact at his house, and found him the same personage, as fresh and delightful as ever, the same charming mixture of benevolence, old-fashioned politeness, simplicity, charity, and love of country life and country pleasures.

And if the good Knight is yet alive, why should we doubt that the courteous readers are yet alive? So I am determined to believe, and that this immortal work will find such readers. There is something so pleasant and mutually honorable to the author and his readers, something so creditable to human nature in the very terms. Courteous Reader! it expresseth the propriety of the relationship between the parties. It expresseth especially the quality of moral fitness on the part of a reader to be a reader. By what other title can he claim? The author taketh pains, doth his best (it is surely seemly always so to presume), to inform or instruct, convince, persuade, entertain, or amuse —in short, in some form to confer benefit or pleasure or both upon his reader. A courteous reception is therefore his due. It is unfit in itself, and it is unbefitting in you to withhold it. As the boor that passeth on with his cap unlifted and untouched, in churlish disregard of the gentle lady that biddeth him good-morrow, so is the reader that cometh not to the perusal of a book in a candid and kindly temper.

A book therefore—always supposing it to be written, as every book should be, in an honest spirit and for a worthy end—a book and a courteous reader are cognate conceptions that should be as inseparable as gentleness and a lady, gallantry and a knight, honor and a gentleman. To put them asunder implies a contradiction.

I have been led into saying all this because I am sensible that I have begun this book in a way that makes some demand upon the courtesy of the reader. I have not begun at the beginning—which is the order of nature; nor at the end; although that is a very possible way to write a book with good effect, and certainly it is an excellent way with some books that are printed to be read from beginning to end, to read them backwards from end to beginning—a thing I shall not quarrel with any reader for doing with this book if ever it come to an end, but rather advise; nor have I begun in the middle of things, which is recommended in some cases.

Now if any one should come blustering up to me with an insolent air and a menacing tone, and demand to know why the —— mischief I opened my book with that chapter on the Library Table before saying any thing about the house, and where it was, and who and what Doctor Oldham was,— in short why I didn't begin at the beginning, I should know the man was not a courteous reader;

and I should decline giving him my reasons upon such compulsion. But to those truly courteous readers, who, taking properly for granted that I have very good reasons, may be desirous at this stage to know what they are, I am cheerfully ready to explain myself.

I did not then begin at the beginning, because when I began I did not know where the beginning was.

I did not begin at the end, because I was equally ignorant when, where, and how it would end, and am so still.

I did not begin in the middle, as Horace advises, because that is the rule for an Epic story, and my book is neither an Epic nor a story.

So much for the reasons why I did *not* begin otherwise than as I did.

Now for the reason why I *did* begin as I did: I put that chapter on the Library Table first, because I wrote it first, and for no other reason that I am aware of.

" But may I ask, sir, why you wrote it first ? "

You may, courteous reader, but that is a point on which I can give you no satisfaction; for I am as ignorant as yourself.

CHAPTER III.

WHICH COMES BETWEEN THE LAST CHAPTER AND THE NEXT ONE.—
THE READER MAY OMIT IF HE WILL; BUT HE WILL LOSE SOMETHING IF HE DOES.

So it is; one thing engenders or draws after it another—be it debt, or blow, or word. I am afraid I shall displease all orderly straight-going people; but it is the penalty of my first false step. Not beginning at the beginning, I involved myself in the necessity of writing that intermediate chapter in order to tell the courteous reader how I came to make the mistake, and to speak him fair. And that leads to another chapter; for it leads to some other things that ought to be said. I might insert them in the middle of the last chapter, cutting it open as they do steamers when they lengthen them. But there's the trouble of it; and, besides, such things are mostly weak-backed and apt to break. So what remains to be said had best be put into a chapter by itself, only let me first take occasion to warn my young readers to remember what consequences are often entailed by a single false step. As with two straight lines starting from the same point with an angle of divergence infinitesimally small. . . . .

"But, sir, will you not be so kind as to proceed at once to the explanation of the things presumed in your first chapter, and then go on with the story?"

O courteous reader—for such I will count you, although your tone is the least in the world peremptory—you are also an impatient reader; and in this very quality you may see the fitness of something further to be said in order that there may be a right understanding between us, and that we may then go on with mutual pleasure, as those who wish to go the same road and wish to go together, or else part company as those who, meeting on the highway, yet bound to different points, hold common course for a brief space with courteous interchange of greeting and remark, until the next fork of the road obliging them to separate, they take leave of each other with mutual respect and good will.

Let me then put you right as to the character of this immortal work, that you may no longer talk about "getting on with the story." Remember, I have said it is not a story at all. It certainly is not, in any proper sense of the word. There is next to nothing of story in it ; and what little there is, is there for the sake of the book, and not the book for the sake of the story—a literary distinction I trust you will not fail to note. The book is a record of talk at Greystones—the talk of Doctor Oliver Oldham. His wife may say something ; his friends may chance to get in a word now and then, but the talk will be mostly the Doctor's, which you may take to be specially implied in the mystic monogram :

It is to be the O. O. book ; not the double nothing book, nor the double odd book, but the Oliver Oldham book—a book full of the Doctor—a book of thought ; for the Doctor is always thinking as well as talking ; and I shall have to set down his thoughts on all sorts of subjects—books and things, men, manners, life, art, morals, politics, and religion.

"Story, God bless you, I have none to tell," as the 'needy knife-grinder' said. You will find it much more a book of sermons than a story. Very queer sermons, too, I dare say you may think some of them; many things in them which Doctor Shallow and Miss Prim will pronounce very nonsensical and foolish, or very irreverent and shocking; and some things, I am afraid, which the Pharisees, Sadducees, and Herodians, will all join in vehement abuse of; but nothing for all that which is not true and salutary to those who know how to receive it—as all truth always is. There will be things solemn, and things facetious, and things out of the common way; but I should not be at the pains to put them down, if I did not think they would be read with pleasure and profit by all the people of my parish—the good and the wise, both those that are grave and those that are gay, and especially those that are both by turns, or (which is best but rarest of all) those that are both at once; and if I did not also hope they would help the young to some right notions, free them from some conventional delusions, cants, and shams, and set up some landmarks of truth and righteousness in the great realm of thought.

Do not, therefore, O curious and impatient

reader, talk of story; neither be over eager for explanations concerning the library that contained the table, and the house that contained the library, and the Doctor, who and what he is that built the house that contained the library, etc., etc. Remember the House that Jack built, and remember, too, the sonnet that Coleridge made on it (after it fell to ruins), showing how small things may be made grand by big words and a sounding style—as may also be seen in the sermons of many of the popular preachers of the day.

Here's the sonnet:

> And this *reft* house is that the which he built,
> Lamented Jack! and here his malt he piled.
> Cautious in vain! these rats that squeak so wild,
> Squeak not unconscious of their fathers' guilt.
> Did he not see her gleaming through the glade!
> Belike 'twas she, the maiden all forlorn,
> What though she milk no cow with crumpled horn,
> Yet aye she haunts the dale where erst she strayed,
> And aye beside her stalks her amorous knight!
> Still on his thighs their wonted brogues are worn,
> And through those brogues, still tatter'd and betorn,
> His hindward charms gleam an unearthly white.
> Ah! thus through broken clouds at night's high noon,
> Peeps in fair fragments forth the full orb'd harvest moon!

Thank me for this sonnet: or if not thankful for it for yourself, try to be thankful I have put it here for those who will be glad to see it, and you may be sure there are some such.

You ought to thank me too for the moral lesson I was going to draw from those two straight lines which you cut off. You cut short a homily which in the compass of a page would have contained more matter for profit to my young and thoughtful readers, than the whole six volumes of Professor Stickinbark's Theological Lectures, or all the Reverend Calvin Grim's awful sermons.

And believe me, O impatient reader, that I never turn aside from what seems to you the straight road, nor ever pause or linger on my way, without good reason,—sometimes for my own pleasure or convenience, but mostly with a view to some special pleasure or advantage which others will find, if you do not. Remember there are others besides thyself, and of more patient mood. Why should the universe be all made over again to suit thy humor? Why all the world be put going sixty miles an hour upon an air-line railway to accommodate thy restless nerves? Why all old country roads destroyed,—no more lanes and byways, no zig-zags, no turnings and windings, no resting places, no summer-houses, nor rustic seats under spreading chestnut or gnarled oak beside the gurgling brook? Is this fair? Is it reasonable? Is it not rather the height of selfishness? Curb, then, this chafing spirit; think more of others and less of yourself. And if you find no pleasure in these intermediate chapters, try to be glad that there are those that will: so shall you yourself get a gain of inestimable value from this very trial of your patience.

As to the rest, let me assure you that while the main interest of this work will be in what the Doctor says, you may look for all needful explanations sooner or later in the coming chapters concerning the Doctor himself, his personal life, and outward circumstances.

CHAPTER IV.

THE LIBRARY NOT MADE FOR THE TABLE.—THE RECESS THAT WAS NOT REALIZED AND THE WINDOW THAT WAS.—THE LIBRARY AS FINISHED.—DOCTOR OLDHAM'S OPINION ABOUT GOOD COMPANY.—HE QUOTES DOCTOR SOUTHEY AND DISCOURSES ABOUT HIM.

THE Library, as well as the table, was a long-cherished ideal of the Doctor's, on which he had set his heart even more than on the table. Indeed, he always asserted that, although the table was made first, yet it was made for the library, and not the library for it.

In giving directions for the library, the Doctor had, as in the matter of the table, gone according to the long looked-at image in his mind's eye, and in the same way of guessing at the dimensions and other details; yet some of the disasters almost inevitably resulting from the difficulty of getting the exact measurement of spiritual images and hitting their proper visible effects, were prevented in this case by the good sense of Mrs. Oldham, who, being

on the spot and daily consulted by the Doctor as
the work went on, luckily prevented more than one
of his images from getting irretrievably realized;
which, however well they might look in an ideal
picture, would have been any thing but satisfactory
in an actual room.

It was, for instance, a part of his ideal to have
a large recessed window at the east end, giving
more expression to the room, and harmonizing better with the west end, which was a semi-octagon
with three windows. And he thought he had an
ingenious contrivance for this; but Mrs. Oldham,
who did not get a clear notion of his plan until
after the studs for the recess were set, pointed out
to him that the effect of it would be to give them
two closets which they did not need, at the expense
of room which they did need. So he gave up his
contrivance and had the studs taken down.

But as for the window, it was too late to alter
that. The Doctor's ideal had got realized, and it
was certainly a mistake. It should have been a
window with three compartments—a wide window
in the middle, and a narrower one on each side,
separated from the larger one by mullions. But it
was made with only two compartments, being in
fact nothing but two ordinary windows set as near

each other as they could be put. The Doctor thought it looked very well in his ideal; but when it got actually made, he became conscious of a secret dissatisfaction with it, which he would not allow himself to analyze or dwell upon, much less breathe a word of to his wife. He hoped indeed she would not see any thing to condemn; but he had an inward dread she might: for, although she had no eye for ideals, her observation of every thing that falls within the scope of ordinary sight was very quick; and, moreover, although entirely unconscious of it herself, she had a wonderful talent for giving exact expression to any secret misgiving he might have, and of suggesting comparisons discreditable to his ideals, without the least intention of wounding him.

Mrs. Oldham had been unable to offer any objection to the window while it was in its ideal state, notwithstanding the Doctor's clearest description of it, for the reason, as I have said, that she had no eye for ideals. But as soon as it became sufficiently real to be visible to her, she said to him:

"Husband, I don't like it. It looks just like a shop-window."

There it was! She had hit the very secret of

his dissatisfaction and made it shockingly palpable. He could no longer shut his eyes to it. That comparison, too! It was just putting his ideal into the pillory, exposing the child of his fancy to irretrievable ignominy. He felt it acutely.

"I wish, my dear," he collected himself at length to say, "I wish you had said so in time to have had it made different."

"I am sure," she replied, "I did not think it was going to look so."

"I think it would perhaps have looked better," said he, fishing for a crumb of consolation, "if we had kept to the original plan about the recess."

"Husband," rejoined Mrs. Oldham, "how would that have altered the shape of the window?"

The Doctor saw she thought the question unanswerable; so he said no more.

He was in the right, however. Even the putting up of the bookcases on each side of the window had something of the same ameliorating effect the recess would have had. And owing partly perhaps to this, and partly to the familiar sight of it, the window soon ceased to trouble Mrs. Oldham; and the Doctor was not one to trouble himself about any thing that did not trouble his wife. He had a favorite dilemma he was very fond of propounding, to the effect that there are two sorts of things a wise man will never trouble himself about —namely, those which he can help, and those which he cannot help. He thought it an infallible recipe against trouble before he was married; but since that event, though he was still as fond as ever of propounding it to his friends, yet somehow he had not the same faith in its universal efficacy, for it did not keep him, as perfectly as it should do, from being troubled at his wife's troubles. It was therefore fortunate for him—and he was sensible of it as a great blessing—that she was not prone to have troubles, and the few she did have were neither very great ones nor lasted very long.

You are to understand, therefore, that on the whole, when everything was completed, the Doctor and his wife regarded their library with mutual satisfaction and content. And it deserved their regard in spite of the window. It was a well-lighted and remarkably cheerful room, fitted up with glazed bookcases on all sides saving the spaces taken up by the windows and by the doors—one opening from the hall, and the other into the Doctor's study. The whole finishing and furnishing was in every respect studiously simple and unpretending; yet every thing was convenient, and the room had an air of thorough comfort and home enjoyment.

This was precisely the expression the Doctor and his wife wished the room to have: for, though fitted up as a library, it was designed to be the living-room of the family—and their drawing-room, too, all they had; there being no proper drawing-room at Greystones. The little parlor on the right of the hall was altogether too small to be called any thing but a reception-room or ladies' morning-room. It was in fact the music-room, for Lilly Oldham had her piano there. The dining-room was a tolerably good-sized one; but the library was the largest room in the house—the only large one—not indeed a grand one, for the ceiling was too low for that; but as to the rest, it would be thought an ample library for a country house of five times the pretension of the Doctor's cottage. Most persons would doubtless have made it the drawing-room, but the Doctor was of a different mind.

"Mrs. Oldham," said he, conversing with his wife before it was built, "we are not rich, and we are not so vulgar as to be ashamed of the fact. Our social consequence, at least in the eyes of all sensible and thorough-bred people, (and they are the only persons for whose opinion we care,) depends on ourselves and not on the money we spend. We can add one large room to our cottage, and only one. Let us not turn that into a show-room for fine furniture, too fine for every-day use. Let us live in it and make it comfortable to live in. Let us fit it up as a library. I don't mean a grand show library for other people's eyes. Our collection is not large enough for my idea of a library of any pretension, and certainly our books are not fine enough in dress for a show library. But let us have our books here, such as we have— my books, yours, and the children's. It is so pleasant to have them always at hand in the room where we mostly live. Here we will pass the evenings together; here receive the friendly neighbors whom we like to have drop in upon us. Here, when by ourselves, we will pass the hours in cheerful chat, or grave discourse, or reading each the book that takes his humor best, or in that highest and finest of social pleasures—a charming book mutually enjoyed. To those who have a taste for good books, how can time ever hang heavy? The winged hours fraught with the present pleasure of delightful studies fly away so swiftly, it would be mournful to consider how swiftly they fly, but that the memory they leave has no sadness in it from the thought they are gone. Many other joys perish in the fruition; this is never a perished joy: such is the marvellous quality of it that not only the past lives in memory, but may be ever renewed with more than its first delight. There is no source of earthly enjoyment that I oftener or more fervently thank God for than that which is to be found in the genial companionship of good books. Let us rejoice, my dear, that we can command here the very highest and best society the world affords. And it is one that has a wonderful advantage over that vulgar product of mushroom wealth which calls itself society in the great town below. We can exclude all the bores and detrimentals of every sort, whether bad in head or bad in heart, or with no heart at all—all the brutes and all the insects, solemn or silly, taciturn or chattering, strutting or fluttering, droning or buzzing, or biting or stinging, that infest ordinary society. We can have our pick out of the finest spirits of every age and nation—all those through whom the world has been made wiser and brighter and better. It is glorious company, those immortal ones! We will cultivate a large acquaintance with them, yet not so large as an intimate one with those we like best. Let us thank God for such choice companionship, always delightful in itself, always at hand, never giving us pain through vanity or caprice, and never changing from friendliness to coldness or ill-will.

"And talking of the companionship of good books reminds me of one I am reading now, and of a passage in it that I marked yesterday. It is in one of Southey's letters to his life-long friend Grosvenor Bedford, and dated from his home among the Cumberland hills just after his settlement there. There is not much in it, but still I was pleased with the feeling it expressed. Here it is:

"'Coleridge is gone for Devonshire, and I was going to say I am alone, but that the sight of Shakespeare, and Spencer, and Milton, and the Bible, on my table, and Castenheda, and Barros, and Ossorio, at my elbow, tell me I am in the best of all possible company.'

"So wrote Southey, at the age of thirty, from that Greta Hall, where, pen in hand, he lived among his books for more than thirty years more, and made the name of his home a familiar and a pleasant name to all who love the memory of a good man and a genuine man of letters. What a love of good books he had. Think of it, my dear—a man without fortune, obliged to write daily for his daily bread, gathering around him more than fourteen thousand choice works, all bought and paid for save those given him by authors and friends. The like case, I guess, cannot be found. And nothing could tempt him away from their companionship. He was made a member of Parliament without his leave asked; but he would not take his seat;—not that he was indifferent to public interests;—no man watched the course of affairs with a keener eye, or did more to give direction to the public mind—as you may see not only in his works published with his name, but in the list of his thirty years' contributions to the Quarterly Review. Nor was it that he felt himself more delightfully at home among his books; but because he thought he could do more good by staying there than in the House of Commons. I must read you his letter about it sometime—so sensible and so good: and I must also read you his letter to Sir Robert Peel, declining the Baronetcy offered him by the king, and the wise and right-hearted reasons he gives.

"Yet Southey's love of books did not make him neglectful of any social or domestic obligation. His widowed mother sustained and cherished by him; his younger brother educated and set forward in an honorable career; his own family creditably maintained, and his children fitted for the best stations in life ; his wife's sisters or sisters' children taken to his hearth and home ;—all this accomplished by the labors of his patient pen, and an honorable independence free from debt ever scrupulously preserved—show him a man fulfilling not only the strict duties, but the noblest charities of domestic life. I declare to you, my dear wife, if God spares my life and health, I should like to write a sketch of the life and writings, the genius, and character of Robert Southey."

"I hope you will do it, husband," said Mrs. Oldham, "it is a beautiful subject, and besides you knew him so well, and he was so kind to you when you were at school in England."

"Ah, if Irving would only give me the pen with which he wrote his charming life of Goldsmith," said the Doctor in reply.

"Why, husband, your pen is good enough : you can do it as well as Mr. Irving, I am sure."

"That is the delusion of an affectionate wife," replied the Doctor ; "but it does credit to your heart, my dear."

CHAPTER V.

GREYSTONES; AND WHAT DOWNING MIGHT HAVE SAID IF HE HAD HAD THE ALTERING OF THE PLAN OF IT.

I THINK we are backing up to the proper starting-place. I begin to have hope we shall, before many chapters, be able to get on in a way more satisfactory to the lovers of regular proceedings. We have gone from the library table to the library. A library (a private library at least, such as the Doctor's) presumes a house of which the library forms a part; that is, if you understand by the word library what I mean, a book-room namely, and not a mere collection of books. The Arabs have fifty words to designate the lion. We have fifty meanings to some single words. I do not object to this. But I think it a grievance that we have not one word exclusively appropriated to denote such an agreeable thing as a comfortable, cheerful room, where one can find good books in plenty, and a plenty of all needful appliances for reading them at ease.

We have now our library: I mean, you and I, courteous reader, have now the Doctor's library—not *implicite*, as before, but *explicite*—no longer as a thing presumed, but a thing set forth. I hope you like it.

But, as I said, the library presumes a house; the house a locality, and some determinate architectural form and fashion—outside looks and inside dispositions; also, environs, prospects, and such like things; and, in fine, also inmates or a family. All these things must be reached by arriving backward in some way, which I am resolved to do in the shortest, that is, the straightest way I may find ability to do it in.

The curious reader is doubtless eager to get at these things. But if he be at the same time an observant and discriminating one, he will notice that the promise is made in such wise only as an honest man, conscious of his peculiar infirmities, will ever make a promise to go straight: it is made with a qualification. I never drink any thing but water, and might safely promise in the most absolute way to keep to the narrowest straight line of literal foot-going ever marked out in space; but as to going a straight line in writing—whether straight forward (which is the natural and proper way), or straight backwards (which is the only right way in this case)—I am so well aware of my propensity to go zig-zaging along to the right and the left, and of the feebleness of my will to resist any temptation that may lure me astray, that I never make any such promise without the reservation proper to one who knows it is an even chance his firmest resolutions may be of no effect. Let us hope for the best. The resolution is an honest one.

The judicious reader will already have noted and put together a number of intimations in the foregoing chapters on all the matters in question; so that I shall only have to fill up what is meagre and to supply what is deficient.

The judicious reader already knows that the Doctor's house is a cottage, and called Greystones. The name was his daughter Lilly's giving. She has a fancy for bestowing pretty and appropriate names upon every thing. She chose this, however, not because she thought it as pretty as some others, but because it was the most appropriate one she could think of. For the house is a low, irregular cottage, of rough-dressed, dark grey stone—the walls covered with ivy, and the pillars of the rustic verandas twined with honeysuckle and other flowering creepers. It is nestled down in a little sheltered nook on the Hudson, a little south of the old Dutch town near which it lies—so near indeed that the Post-office, the churches, and shops, are all within ten minutes' walk. Yet it is shut out from the view of the town by one of two small hills, which look as though they were once only one single hill, in shape like an inverted bowl, that had been split down in the middle and shoved apart, so as to form a little triangular valley with a wide opening towards the river, while at the apex or smallest end the faces of the split hill come so near together as to leave only an opening for a road into the tiny valley. The faces of these twin hills are almost perpendicular crags, with a few small cedars, dogwood, and other shrubs and wild-vines growing out of the seams and fissures of the rocks. The other sides are gentle acclivities clothed with cedars of some size.

At the narrow end of this secluded little hollow, on the right hand as you enter it by the road between the hills, near the face and under the shelter of the one that looks to the south-west, stands the cottage. The little hollow is, however, high up above the level of the river, on the edge of the ridge, that runs back with a pretty sharp ascent from the water-side for nearly a mile before you reach the plateau where the town mostly lies; so that, although it is shut in by the hills that flank it on the eastern side, it commands a view, not only of the hills across the river, doubling and trebling their outlines against the western sky, but to the south of a long reach of the river and the Fishkill mountain, that seems to bar all further progress of the water on its journey to the sea;—while away up in the far north-west the Shawangunk and the Catskill mountains loom up—their sides relieved against the sky mostly by a darker blue, but often (in the winter) by a covering of white.

Greystones had undergone some alterations since the Oldhams came there. They found the cottage quite small, and the rooms, with the exception of the one they set apart for the dining-room, were not only of very tiny dimensions, but there were not enough of them for the accommodation of the family; so that the Doctor had to set immediately about enlarging his new home. And what with erections put alongside and erections put on top, it soon straggled out into a very anomalous edifice, with all sorts of heights of stories and sky outlines; yet within, it had a plenty of just such rooms as were wanted, and in just such connection with each other as they should be for the convenience of the family—not omitting the little study off the library, with the bath-room and dressing-room adjoining, which were the Doctor's special contrivance for his own particular convenience.

Doctor Oldham had been his own architect, and thinking of nothing at first but how to secure the proper number and connection of rooms, had drawn some ground-plans, and set the builder to work upon them—leaving the whole matter of external effect to make the best bargain it could afterwards with himself and the builder, who was only a common carpenter, and the farthest in the world from a Downing or an Upjohn. So the result was something not likely to be copied into any book of designs for model cottages.

But within, it was so roomy, comfortable, and cheerful, that the Doctor was perfectly contented with his dwelling; and would have been so, even if the outside had been ever so queer in the estimation of his out-door neighbors, provided its inmates were satisfied with it. But Mrs. Oldham liked it; Phil liked it; Lilly liked it; Fred liked it; and

Cousin Kitty liked it—they all liked it as a whole, and each their own rooms in particular.

Nor are you to understand that the cottage is at all what could be called grotesque or ugly. It is merely something a little out of the common way in its appearance. But it has a certain agreeable harmony of its various parts, and a pleasing unity as a whole—expressive especially of a thoroughly modest and unpretending union of snugness and sufficiency, amplitude and comfort. And though so near to the town, and with but a few acres of domain, yet, what with being screened from it as they are, and with the wide and beautiful views they can command, the family have all that sense of rural life, that feeling of being in the country, which they love so much, and so largely enjoyed at Oldwood.

As I like you, O courteous and friendly reader, to have a clear and vivid image of every thing imageable relating to the Doctor, I have sketched the ground plan of his cottage somewhat after Downing's fashion—which I dare say you will be pleased to study a little. The elevation and perspective of the exterior, I cannot draw ; but I intend to get one of the Doctor's artist friends, Weir or Withers, to make sketches of it, both as seen from the foot of the lawn, and also from the east, as you first come in sight of it, when you enter the grounds by the road. The plan shows the rooms on the first floor; of the second, I give no sketch — the reader will please to imagine it divided into a sufficient number of convenient bedrooms. He will also bear in mind that the vestibule or entrance-porch is on the east side of the house; the other side faces toward the river, and commands the views I have mentioned.

This ground plan is one which I am apt to think the lamented Downing himself would not have disdained to consider. Indeed, I am ready to believe he would have pronounced it, in several respects, a very commendable plan. I presume he would have somewhat altered the disposition of the rooms. He might have made the library smaller — at all events he would have had a drawing-room; either converting the present library to that purpose, and taking the dining-room for a library, or else taking the dining-room for a drawing-room — in which case he would have lengthened it at the west end, putting in a large bay window; and in either case, he would have taken Mrs. Oldham's room for a dining-room, enlarging it somewhat, and providing a room for her up-stairs. This done,

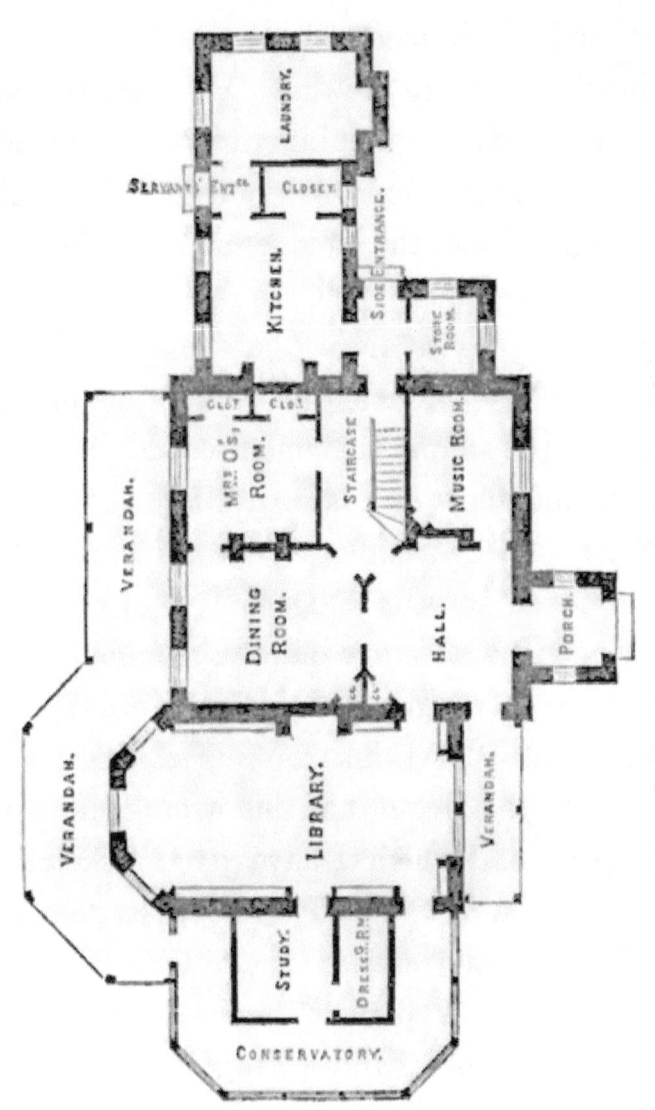

I think he would have written something on this wise : "A sensible, unpretending house ; a judicious and convenient disposition of the rooms. Nothing appears to be wanting to the accommodation and comfort of the inmates, who are evidently persons of refinement and culture. The size of the library shows the predominance of intellectual tastes in the family, and the general appearance of the interior—its dispositions and arrangements, indicate a love for domestic life, for refined pleasures, and the simple enjoyments of a quiet country home in the midst of a beautiful nature."

So, I say, the lamented Downing might have written ; and it is as perfectly true of the Doctor's house and the Doctor's family, as though he had altered the plan in the way I have supposed he might. Indeed, I think the remarks better apply to the plan the Doctor and his wife fixed upon and carried out, and which I have given a sketch of for the inspection of the reader who takes pleasure in considering such plans. I am fond of studying them myself. I like to read Downing's books on country houses and cottages, and landscape gardening ; and I think we in this country owe him a great debt of gratitude—for he has done more than any other person to awaken and extend a taste for the beautiful in a direction which eminently tends to the improvement of the people in true culture, in happiness, and in goodness.

In considering this plan, the reader will please to note that the Doctor's study is a lean-to, built against the library, and is lighted from the roof. This allows the conservatory to be built around it in the way indicated in the sketch. In cold weather, a hot-water apparatus in the cellar warms the conservatory, the study, and the library— although in the latter a fire is also kept in the grate for its cheerful looks.

The consideration of this plan, as a whole, and especially the largeness of the library, the little study, the conservatory, the absence of a drawing-room proper, the music-room—in short, all the details will tell the judicious and thoughtful reader a good deal about the Doctor and his wife—their dispositions and tastes, and the ways and habits of the family.

Thus it often is that things which at first glance seem to be mere facts, dead and barren, become living, seminal, and fruitful—to those who think.

> "O reader! had you in your mind
> Such stores as silent thought can bring:
> O gentle reader! you would find
> A tale in every thing."

CHAPTER VI.

HENRY REED.—COLERIDGE ON WORDSWORTH'S VERSES.—THE DOCTOR'S THEORY OF THE DISTINCTION BETWEEN MAN AND THE BRUTES, AND ALSO OF THE EDIBLE AND POTABLE UNIVERSE, AS PROPOUNDED TO PROFESSOR CLARE.

HENRY REED, Wordsworth's friend and genial editor, whose name calls up to the fancy of all who knew and loved him (and all loved him who knew him) the image of a man of most refined culture, of most intimate acquaintanceship with every thing choice in literature and art, of most pure and perfect taste and judgment for every thing graceful and beautiful, true and good ; and more than all this, of a beauty of character such as is seldom seen and never surpassed—manly virtue (planting itself firmly on the ground of clearly seen principle to stand and withstand) united to a womanly tenderness and delicacy of moral feeling and a womanly quickness and rectitude of moral sentiment ;—whose name recalls also the terrible images of that afternoon of the 27th of September, 1854, when the ill-fated Arctic and her three hundred passengers (he among them) went down to a watery grave—images that will be ever vivid in the fancy of those who had dearly loved friends on board, although they have doubtless now grown dim in most others' minds (such is the effect of time, and of the intensity of our times, and the continual recurrence of similar catastrophes, the last one effacing the memory of the one that went before); whose name is now so well and widely known, by those who knew him not when in life, through those exquisite products of his mind, those fruits of his academic studies and labors, which the hand of fraternal piety has given to the world—not all it will give, let us hope, now that the Chinese embassy is ended ;—HENRY REED has a note upon those lines of Wordsworth which I have given at the end of the last chapter. It is in his edition of the poet's works. It is mostly indeed a quotation from Coleridge ; and it is that quotation which I wish to quote, but as I quote it from Henry Reed's quotation, I cannot do so without being thus reminded of him—what he was, and of the way of his sad loss to the world. Peace to the memory of one of the best and gentlest of men !

"To have formed the habit," says Coleridge, "of looking at every thing not for what it is relative to the purposes and associations of men in general, but for the truths which it is suited to represent—to contemplate objects as *words* and pregnant symbols;—the advantages of this are so many, and so important, and so eminently calculated to excite and evolve the power of sound and connected reasoning, of distinct and clear conception, that there are few of Wordsworth's finest passages—and who of living poets can lay claim to half the number?—that I repeat so often as that homely quatrain:

> "O reader! had you in your mind
> Such stores as silent thought can bring;
> O gentle reader! you would find
> A tale in every thing."

Now the habit signalized by Coleridge is an eminent quality and a characteristic trait of the Doctor's mind. The universe of matter is to him only matter for reflection. He finds no interest in mere dead facts. To him indeed most facts are living, seminal, fruitful, or if not that, at least suggestive; but, if neither—if utterly dead and barren—they are to him as nothing.

The Doctor has however a way of talking sometimes, which I cannot quite commend—particularly to Professor Clare, whose face often gets a very puzzled look in listening to him: indeed, it takes a man who understands the Doctor to understand precisely what and how much of serious meaning there sometimes is in his talk—how much is intended for sense and how much for nonsense. An instance which occurred the other day will illustrate this, as well as that quality of the Doctor's mind, which I have remarked upon above.

Professor Clare happened to stay to dinner with them that day. They had roasted goose on the table; and that set the Doctor off—not on a wild-goose chase, but on a flight into the regions of speculation touching the origin and significance of many of the old customs, such as the Christmas Goose, Shrovetide Pancakes, Good Friday Hot Cross Bunns, and Easter or Paschal Eggs.

He had stuck the fork in the right place, but the carving-knife lay idly in his grasp, resting on the goose it should have been employed in cutting up.

Mrs. Oldham and the children watched his flight,—Mrs. Oldham placidly, Lilly and Cousin Kitty with amused resignation, Phil and Fred with the comical expression of hungry boys trying to behave properly under trying circumstances. What Professor Clare thought could not be told. He listened with an air of great interest.

"Husband," interposed Mrs. Oldham, after a little while, "hadn't you better help us to something to eat?"

She said this in her placid way, without the least rebuke or sarcasm in tone or intention; and so the Doctor understood her.

"Oh! Ah! Yes, my dear," said he, beginning to carve the goose, "I will postpone my remarks. It is ill-preaching to hungry folks; for as the incomparable Pantagruel saith to Panurge, 'it is a most difficult thing for the spirits to be in a good plight, serene and lively, when there is nothing in the body but a kind of voidness and inanity; seeing that the philosophers with the physicians jointly affirm'" . . . .

The Doctor by this time had stopped carving. Lilly and Kitty exchanged glances, amused but not derisive (for they both held the Doctor in great love and reverence); while Phil and Fred could hardly restrain the expression of their impatience. It was lucky for them their mother interposed again. She was the children's providence, the Doctor's good genius in general, and his gentle *flapper* in especial, in cases like this. And it was in the word "husband," by which she always addressed him, and in the way she spoke it, that the charm seemed to lie.

"Husband," said she, gently interrupting him at this point, "you have not helped us yet."

"Bless me, no more I have, my dear," replied the Doctor, coming fully to himself, "but I will help you all now and myself too, and we will eat our dinner before I say any thing more."

He kept his word this time. A lively discussion of good things followed; but altogether of a literal and practical sort.

But as they were returning to the library, he began:

"Professor Clare," said he, "can you think that roasted goose and plum-pudding, turkeys and mince-pies, are merely food for the body? Are they not also food for the mind? As also all things edible and potable?"

"It may be so," replied the Professor, "in the sense of your Pantagruel, whose remark you quoted: the functions of our minds depend upon our bodies, and our bodies depend upon food. A man starved to death will not make much display of mind, nor a man faint from hunger a very lively one."

"But that is not the sense I mean," said the Doctor; "that is altogether a mere Pantagruelian view: it is of the earthly understanding, earthly. No, sir; my opinion is that all things eatable and drinkable are food for the mind, through the capacity of the soul to be thereby prompted and lifted up to spiritual reflections, as multifarious as the objects of the gustatory universe. Herein, in fact, lies the main distinction between man and the brute, and the only real eminence of the former over the latter in the matter of eating. Does it not seem so to you?"

"But some philosopher has made a different distinction," said the Professor, "and defined man as a 'cooking animal.'"

"Do you happen to know the name of that philosopher?" inquired the Doctor.

"No," replied the Professor.

"Neither do I," returned the Doctor, "but I hold him in small respect, whatever his name may be. Pretty philosopher, to find the distinguishing characteristic of man in an accident, which, even if it be an inseparable accident, does not come within a hundred miles of beginning to vindicate for human beings the attribute of reason!

"Besides, cooking or not cooking, is altogether

an affair of the palate—a matter of preference: there is no room even for mooting the question of rationality about it—*de gustibus non est disputandum,* you know. It is equally rational for the Welshman to like toasted cheese as it is for me to dislike it. And so it is just as rational for the lion to like his beefsteak raw as it is for the Englishman to like it underdone, or the Frenchman thoroughly done with truffle sauce,—full as human for the cat to take its rat uncooked, as for the Chinaman to cook his rat before he takes it.

"Nothing, my dear sir, can be argued from such differences of taste. The crow is fond of uncooked carrion, the Fejee islander of baked man. Is the crow's taste less rational? Would a preference for cooked carrion make a man of the crow? Would the Fejee islander cease to be a man, if he should come to like a piece of raw missionary better than a cut of cold roast? Will anybody maintain this?"

"But may it not be questioned whether it is merely a matter of taste?" interposed the Professor; "is it not the ingenuity shown in cooking his food that the philosopher had in mind, when he made his definition?"

"Well, granting it to be so," replied the Doctor, "is ingenuity in material adaptations an attribute belonging exclusively to rational beings? No, sir, that cannot be maintained. If it could, it would only prove that there are rational brutes. For I am bold to affirm that the way in which many sorts of animals take and store away their food which they do not cook, shows vastly more sagacity than some tribes of human beings display in their modes of cooking their food."

"All instinct," suggested the Professor.

"No, sir," said the Doctor, "what I refer to cannot be called instinct. There are, it is true, very many wise doings of brutes that are matters of pure instinct—blind instinct, as all pure instinct always is. This sort of doings the animals that do them do not know the wisdom of;—it is not their wisdom but their Maker's, that works in them by a law in their nature which leads them to do those things always invariably in the same way under all circumstances, and as perfectly the first as the thousandth time—as, for instance, the ways in which the different sorts of birds always build their nests. That is instinct. It is not of that I was speaking, but of cases where animals will vary their conduct as circumstances vary, adapt their contrivances to sudden exigencies, take different means to-day from those they took yesterday to accomplish the same end, because they find themselves in different conditions. This is not instinct. I do not say it is reason. I do not believe it is. But it is skill, it is sagacity, it is intelligence; and it is the animal's own intelligence, their Maker's intelligence, indeed, considered as the gift of a faculty—and so is ours—but their own intelligence, as not working blindly and always in the same way, which instinct does.

"If you would know all about this wonderful ingenuity of animals, go read Huber on Bees and on Ants—very remarkable books to be written by a blind man; but he used his wife's eyes to see with (I believe), and his wife's pen to make the record; and that is the reason, no doubt, why the books are at once so wise and so charmingly agreeable. Read, too, almost any of the books that tell us of the fox, the beaver, the elephant, and the dog, and you will confess that the ingenuity of many animals, in taking and storing their food, is greater than the cooking ingenuity of some human tribes.

"So you see it will not do to defend that philosopher's definition on the score of the ingenuity evinced by man as a cooking animal. Ingenuity is not rationality; and if it were, there are many species of brutes more rational than some men are."

"No, sir," continued the Doctor, "it is not because he cooks his food that man is man; nor is it any more because of any superior nicety of taste and neatness in his ways.

"Such distinctions are arbitrary; you cannot draw the line.

"With what show of justice can you exclude the quadruped that feeds on swill, or the feathered biped that is fond of carrion, from the category of rational beings, and yet include the Germans who eat sauer-kraut, the Esquimaux who are fond of whale-blubber, or the Laplanders who esteem putrid eggs fried in train-oil a special delicacy—which latter fact I mention, not as of my own knowledge or reading, but on the authority of my friend Doctor Wilton, who is very seldom mistaken, and thinks he never is.

"There are crows that like their fresh meat to lie by until it has acquired a game flavor. So does Alderman Gubbins—he always has his wild-fowl and venison laid aside until it is quite—tender. Is not the similarity of taste undeniable?"

"But there is a wide difference between them for all that," said the Professor.

"I admit there is a difference of degree," replied the Doctor. "I will admit, if you wish—

though I, for my part, do not see it—that the German taste is more human than the Esquimaux or Laplanders' taste, and the latter more so than the taste of swine and crows; but in degree only. And will you make the distinction between man and the brutes a mere matter of degree?

"The pig thrusts his snout clear to the bottom of his wooden trough, and roots and nudges its contents about with a grunt and gurgle of satisfaction. The little pig eyes of Alderman Gubbins twinkle with equal satisfaction—and of the same sort, as he ladles his turtle-soup out of a silver tureen and ladles it into his mouth with a gold spoon. Is it in the difference between swill and turtle-soup, or between the wooden trough and the silver tureen, or between putting one's nose into it or using a golden spoon—is it in these things, or in any of them, that you would find the essential difference between the pig and Alderman Gubbins. You surely cannot maintain this.

"No, my dear Professor, it is in the capacity to reflect upon what he eats, to ascend to the spiritual by means of the sensible, and so to derive from the food of the body a nourishment for the soul—it is in this that the difference between man and the brute consists; and only so far as he does this, is Alderman Gubbins superior to the pig."

Professor Clare's face had, for some time, worn a puzzled look. So he made no reply—only he asked for the volumes of Huber, which he took, and shortly after went away.

"Husband," said Mrs. Oldham, when he was gone, "you sometimes put off so much nonsense upon Professor Clare. Why do you do it?"

"Well, my dear," replied the Doctor, "there was a great deal of sense in it, as well as some nonsense—and truth, too, not of the smallest order, although some of the logic was no better than it should be—which is partly what puzzled Professor Clare. Comfort yourself, however: it will lead him to read those charming books, and so be the occasion of his gaining a great delight."

I have given the Doctor's notion in regard to the edible universe; but it was not of that alone he thus thought: the whole universe of matter was to him mere matter for reflection (as I have said before), and in a sort transfigured thereby.

CHAPTER VII.

SHORT, IF NOT SWEET.—DIFFERENCE BETWEEN THE AUTHOR AND RABELAIS, AND SOME OTHER CELEBRATED WRITERS.

THE curious reader is doubtless now expecting me to go on, and give him the personal history of the Doctor and his family; because that is the next thing in order, according to the virtuous resolution of going straight backward to the beginning, which I recorded in the chapter before the last.

I have not, I confess, a very high respect for that inquisitive eagerness to get at the personal history of everybody they see, which is so marked a trait in the character of some of my acquaintances.

There is, however, one direction of this curiosity which I have a very cordial sympathy with. It is natural we should take a lively interest in knowing every thing relating to the personal history and character of those writers that have greatly delighted us and done us good—those benefactors to our minds and hearts to whom we owe great debts of acknowledgment, we can never pay here below; whose names "breed in us perpetual benediction." The impulse to gather up every incident of their earthly lives, every trait and trace of their habits and ways, is spontaneous, and it is as creditable to the heart as it is natural.

A feeling similar to this, will, I have no doubt, be very strong in regard to Doctor Oldham, in the hearts of a multitude of the readers of this book, long before they come to the end of it, if ever it come to an end. But at present it can hardly have begun to spring up. It seems to me it would be time enough to gratify it when it has grown fervent—when the sense of delight and benefit received from the many wise and beautiful utterances of his, which it will be my duty to record, shall have raised their love and admiration to the proper pitch. It would seem to me then a most laudable curiosity, which I should find pleasure in gratifying so far as I could do it with propriety.

There are limits to such things. The Doctor is yet alive, and would never permit me to make this book the pretext and means of thrusting before the public the trivialities of his daily life—chronicling the names and ages of his cats and dogs and horses, and their ways and doings—unless there was something really remarkable in them; opening the doors of his dressing-room, and displaying his shavings and washings, the sort of soap and towels he prefers, his dentrifice, tooth-brushes, and back-scratcher, and other intimacies of his private ways—such as Rabelais, in his great unconscious simplicity and plainness of speech, might disclose to all the world, but which the Doctor would no more consent to have done than I should be willing to do. There is now and then a celebrated writer of our days, who is willing to do this for himself, and for other celebrities too, if he gets a chance. But let the Doctor's privacy be sacred until he is dead. Then let any foolish Boswell (not me) disclose what he will, so it be true: it will not impair the venerableness of the Doctor in good men's thoughts. For myself, I shall present the Doctor to the public only in such guise as he shows himself to all who may chance to be at his house. As to the rest, I shall not withhold any thing that may happen to fall from his lips relating to his past life, which I may have reason to think he would be willing to communicate to any inquiring friend. I make no doubt the reader, if he be a judicious and not over-curious one, will be able to put together enough for his satisfaction.

I may as well say here that the Doctor is a man a little above the middle height—well built, though stout, and now somewhat inclining to fulness of habit. His large head is covered with a profusion of soft, curling hair, once light brown, but now turned nearly white. He has large, clear, light blue eyes; but he is quite near-sighted, and always wears glasses. His complexion is fair and ruddy, and his countenance has an expression at once thoughtful and benignant—betokening a man of good sense and good humor, of a joyous and genial social temper—which is eminently the quality of the Doctor's nature; though he is apt to fall into fits of absent-mindedness, particularly when the speculative cast of his mind and the peculiar associations of his thoughts lead him off in some odd out of the way track. This it is which makes him so prone to dissertate rather than converse.

CHAPTER VIII.

THE DOCTOR VISITS MRS. ROSSVILLE'S SCHOOL.—AND TELLS HIS WIFE WHAT HE SAID TO THE LITTLE FOLKS THERE. — MR. GRIM. — HOW GOD TAKES CARE THE CHILDREN SHALL NOT BE HURT BY BAD CATECHISMS.

"I HAVE been up to Mrs. Rossville's school," said the Doctor to his wife one evening. "It was a sort of anniversary, when the children get each a present of some nice book suitable to their age and intelligence. Why, Mrs. Rossville and the other ladies have gathered together more than sixty children, in that outlying district, who would otherwise be very poorly off for needful instruction."

"Yes," said the Doctor's wife, "Mrs. Rossville's heart is full of love and kindness towards everybody, and especially those who need any thing she can do for their welfare. That neighborhood has reason to be glad she is so rich, and has so much in her power."

"True," replied the Doctor, "and her face is as full of sunshine and joyousness as her heart is of love and kindness, and this, together with her simple, unaffected, good-natured ways and words, has such a magnetic charm for the little folks that, combined with their delight in their presents, the room was positively filled with a perfect glory of sunshine and gladness. I declare it was really beautiful to see them all standing up, the smallest ones in front—and rows of bright faces rising one above the other behind, and blending their voices—tiny, tinier, and tiniest, but all joyous and hearty voices—in a hymn:

> All things bright and beautiful,
>   All creatures great and small;
> All things wise and wonderful,
>   The Lord God made them all.

The music was not absolutely perfect in time and tune, but it really was not the worse for that; nor was every figure in the group as beautiful and graceful as Greenough's Chanting Cherubs—though there were faces there as fine as any Greenough ever dreamed of; but the whole effect was high above any art of sculptor or painter to produce."

"But what did you say to the children, husband?"

"Well, I dare say it would have seemed very queer talk to many persons; it would have made Mr. Grim look more grim, and Miss Prim more prim, if they had been there. But I told the children I was glad to see them so glad about their books—that children did not formerly have so many books as they have now, but I was not sure they were any the worse off; for the few they had were better read, and so did them more good,— while now they had so many there was danger they would read more than they could read in a way to make their minds grow;—that it was a great deal better to read a few books over and over, again and again, than to run hastily through a great many; —and, besides, there were a great many books for children nowadays, written with a very good intention, that were very poor stuff—not half so good for them as some of those old ones which some very wise people now think so foolish: that Mother Goose's Melodies, and Cock Robin, and Jack o' the Bean Stalk, and Jack the Giant Killer, and Cinderella, and Beauty and the Beast, and Æsop's Fables with the Cuts, and Berquin's Children's Friend, and the Treasury of Choice Old Fairy Tales, and the Story of Poor Joseph, and Robinson Crusoe, and Sinbad the Sailor, were a library for little folks which none of the wise modern books could make up for the want of—and I was glad to see them among their books; though some of the new books were indeed as wise and good for them as any thing that could possibly be imagined—such as Hans Andersen's Stories, and Masterman Ready, and the Settlers in Canada, and Sir Edward Seward's Narrative, and that exquisite little book, A Trap to Catch a Sunbeam, and other equally beautiful stories by the same hand, and the Boy Missionary, and the Ministering Children, and some others that I could name—and I was glad to see them among the books to-day; only this they must remember, that the more they read such books as the last two, the more dead their consciences would become, and the harder their hearts, if they did not try in some way, according to their opportunities, to imitate the good examples which touched their tender feelings so deeply;—and as to the rest, they must have nothing to do with such books as Professor Savethought's Truth Brought Down, his Philosophy Made Easy, and Great Things Made Small; nor with Mr. Silley's Series: the Child's Book of Physiology, of Natural Theology, and the rest; nor with Mrs. Softly's Childish Hymns; nor Mrs. Scarem's Awfulness of Infant Sin, and Sad

Fate of the Little Sabbath Breakers, nor Miss Sharp's Profitableness of Piety—showing the wisdom of serving God because He pays better than the Evil One;—that they must never look into those books; and, in fine, they must speak the truth, obey their parents, love their brothers and sisters, be kind to everybody, say their prayers, and remember always that they were God's children and not the Devil's; and that God loved to see them play if they played fair, and loved to have them have a good time playing as often as they could get it, provided they did not neglect any duty or do any thing wrong;—that they should always try to do right because it was right, and not merely for any thing they might hope to gain by it, whether from God or from others; and never to do wrong because it was wrong, and not merely from fear of what might come of it either here or hereafter;—that the Good Lord loved them dearly, and had not a thought or a wish about them, but to have them good, and happy here and forever, and they should therefore live as His dear children, and try to please Him out of love;—that they could not be good without His help, any more than they could lift themselves over the river in a basket;—that it was sometimes hard to be good, harder for some than for others, because their nature was not as favorable, (some being naturally more prone than others to get angry or out of patience, or to be sullen or resentful, or vain, or proud, or selfish and self-willed, or idle and unsteady,) but God did not think any the worse of them on that account, provided they honestly tried to be good; indeed, the harder they found it, the more God was pleased with them, if only they tried the more earnestly;— and they must not be discouraged, or afraid of God, if they should sometimes stumble and fall into wrong (as most likely they would), but be sorry, and keep on striving to do right, and be sure that God would then love them just as tenderly, and forgive them, and make all allowance for them, just as loving fathers and mothers always do, and they would certainly succeed at last, for God's Good Spirit was in all their hearts to help every one to become good that honestly tried, and kept on trying.

"There, Mrs. Oldham, that is the substance of my talk to the little folks—not a phonographic record, but a pretty fair report—and how do you like it?"

"I think it is very good," said she, "but it sounds very different from Mr. Grim's preaching.

He speaks of God in such a way as to frighten children from trusting Him, and so makes it impossible for them to love Him; they cannot help thinking of Him as austere, morose, and terribly strict — a foe to all innocent mirth and merriment."

"It is all along of his mistaken notions of goodness," replied the Doctor, "and partly of his natural temper, and partly of his unhappy instruction, that he has such mistaken notions. He mistakes sanctimony for saintliness, strictness for religiousness; and so it is nothing strange he should have a God after the fashion of such ideas. His way of representing God was once characterized by one of a company of soldiers, after I had been speaking to them of God's love for them notwithstanding the low rank they held in the estimation of men, and however deeply they might have fallen in moral degradation. The man thanked me for what I had said, observing that most of those who preached to them, spoke as if Christ might be their friend, but they must beware of God.

"I told him I was sorry they should ever be so taught.

"'Sir,' said he, 'they make God a *Police Sergeant!*'"

"That was the poor fellow's own title and function at the post where his troop was stationed."

"What is the function?" asked Mrs. Oldham.

"To keep a sharp look-out on the men, and bring them up for punishment for all neglect or infraction of orders," replied the Doctor.

"But how good God is. At first thought it would seem one of the mournfullest things in the world that the little folks should be deprived of the sweet influence of right instruction—the blessed sense that they are God's dearly-loved children, and subjected to such teaching as Mr. Grim's—made to think themselves the children of the Evil One, and sure to fall into his clutches at the last, unless they should happen to be among the elect—which it was ten to one they were not. One would think their young life would be overshadowed and chilled to its very centre, by the great black horror of such a creed.

"But God takes care it shall not be so.

"If you chance to come upon a troop of those little ones out of doors at school recess, you will see them running, and scampering, and kicking up their heels like young colts let loose, and filling the air with the merry ring of their shouts and laughter. A strange spectacle and a frightful one

—in a right logical consideration of the creed they are taught—to see the doomed little wretches so joyous and thoughtless amidst the terrific chances of their fate!

"But God, the true loving God, is stronger in their hearts than their Catechism, setting forth a God worse than none, by all the difference between a bad one and none.

"Let us rejoice it is so.

"Let us be thankful that such unwholesome instructions enter so little into the life circulation of children's hearts, but roll off, for the most part, like the little pellets of hail from the windows, without any adhesion at all."

"But, husband, do you think that the parents and elders really hold any such terrible doctrines?"

"Well, they think they do; some of them only think they do, but in reality do not—they hold only the words; some perhaps hold the doctrines, but without seeing or believing in the consequences. Which is another blessed thing. Then, too, being fathers and mothers has a wonderful influence: it is one of God's contrivances in behalf of little children. He takes care that there shall be a blessed inconsistency between a mother's head and a mother's heart, between a father's creed and a father's love : and so through God's love in them and their parents' love surrounding them, the little ones get a chance for a joyous childhood—unless in the midst of very unhappy outward circumstances. O when will all those be friendly ! I never think of the social life of highly civilized nations, with so much sorrow for its evils in any of its other relations, as in its bearing upon the unfolding of childhood."

CHAPTER IX.

MORE TALK ABOUT CHILDREN.—THE GOOD LORD'S CONTRIVANCES TO PREVENT THEIR BEING SHUT OUT OF THE WORLD OF FICTION.

Mrs. Oldham had been sitting for some time in silence, her scissors busily running in and out the indented edge of a collar she was trimming for Lilly. Fred and his sister were on the other side of the table, each absorbed in reading—the one Ivanhoe, the other Miss Yonge's beautiful tale of Heart's Ease. The Doctor was looking over the newspaper.

"Husband," said Mrs. Oldham at length, casting her eyes upon the children, "how different the feeling among good people now from what it used to be about novels and works of fiction."

"Yes," replied the Doctor, "they did not understand, in the days of your grandmother, that it is through the world of fiction children first enter into the divine and eternal world."

"Dear me! husband, I am afraid I don't understand you," returned his wife.

"I beg your pardon, my dear; I was absurdly transcendental in phrase. I mean that it is from true fiction—from the living products of the creative imagination, children get their first ideas of the wonderful, of a world out of nature, the supernatural and divine. True and pure fiction is the purest truth—the natural and necessary aliment for the young imagination, through the quickening of which faculty alone the other faculties of mind and heart are best unfolded, even if they can be at all unfolded in any other way."

"A sad time then, in those old days, for the unfolding of the young mind and heart," said Mrs. Oldham; "almost a hopeless case."

"So one would say at first thought," replied the Doctor; "but God watches over the little ones. He contrives compensations and protections where they are concerned. He does not let monstrous doctrines and pious absurdities of prejudice altogether prevail over common sense and the impulses of love in parents' hearts.

"In those days children were indeed made to study the Westminster Catechism for their Sunday (or as they called it Sabbath) lessons. Robinson

Crusoe would have been much better Sunday reading for them; they would really have gotten something from it—something good and quickening to true religious feeling in their hearts. But then, God be thanked, neither the children nor, for the most part, their parents understood the Catechism: so the harm was small—rather in the good they did not get than in the harm they did.

"But (as I said) there were compensations for the little people. For the younger ones the Primer, which contained the Catechism, contained many things besides—things that young and healthy minds could contrive to grow upon. There was that wonderful alphabet with its picture and couplet of verses to each letter, of which I remember nothing bad but the opening:

<blockquote>
In Adam's Fall,
We sinned all.
</blockquote>

"This might have done the children harm if they had understood and believed, or tried to believe the meaning it was framed to convey, or at least it might have perplexed and troubled their young thoughts. But I don't think they got any insight of that meaning, and so no harm; nor would they, I think, if the couplet had been turned into a quatrain by adding—what might with equal truth be added:

> In **C**ain his Murthur,
> We sinned further.

"There too was the moving ballad of the burning of John Rogers, and the still more moving picture of his wife and nine small children around him at the stake—the children's heads going down just like the steps of stairs from biggest to least, except the littlest one that was carried at the mother's breast. Other things there were too in that Primer which (without any purpose or consciousness, you may be sure, on the part of its makers) had the genial effect of good fiction on the childish mind and heart.

"Then, too, the children, both younger and older, had the range of the Bible—perhaps the great Family Bible, containing sometimes most remarkable wood cuts or engravings, and even perhaps the Apocrypha, a marvellous addition to their treasures, although some of them were not allowed to read it on the Sabbath. The Bible! full of stories—all novels and tales to children—some of them indeed not so suitable and salutary for children as Robinson Crusoe and other novels that might be named, but very many of them of such beauty and interest as no other book can surpass: the stories of Joseph; of Ruth; of Little Samuel; of David and Goliath; of Daniel; of Jonah;—and those parables of our Lord, the Good Samaritan and the Prodigal Son, which make little people's eyes fill up and run over with sympathetic tears, so much do they quicken the imaginative faculty and touch the heart.

"Then for week days there was the blessed nonsense of Mother Goose's Melodies, which the Good Lord (I cannot but think) took special care, through his hold on the instincts of mothers' hearts, that no black doctrines of predestination and decrees, and no puritanical sourness of sanctimony should deprive the little ones of; and as they grew bigger, there were Æsop's Fables, with those wonderful woodcuts, in the Spelling Books, where were stories too—such as the story of Poor Joseph (who had so many children to feed and so little to feed them with) and his little boy, who thought he would not eat his share of the bread, but die and go to God, that there might be more for his brothers and sisters—a story that has drawn many a tear from many eyes;—and other stories, more than I can mention—all of them novels and tales and romances to the young. Besides this—and it seems to have been a special 'dispensation of Providence' in favor of the young—it almost always happened, in some mysterious way, by nobody's procurement in particular, there went circulating through every neighborhood, stray copies of Cinderella or the Glass Slipper, Beauty and the Beast, the Transformations of Indus, Aladdin's Wonderful Lamp, and Sinbad's Voyages, which somehow the pious fathers and mothers failed to see belonged to the class of books prohibited; and so the little ones got those ideas of the wonderful and supernatural which, entering the childish mind through the imagination, in the garb of fiction, prepare it for divine eternal truths. Then too, God be thanked, there were but few children, in New England at least, that did not in some way, through His contrivance, get hold of Robinson Crusoe—the most fascinating of human books to children at a proper age; of the reading whereof observant persons would find proof in numberless islands, not surrounded by water, where shipwrecked little people built huts and played at Crusoe and his man Friday with great delight, while their minds unfolded and grew in the joyous activity of their play.

"So it may be seen what providences and

what compensations there were for children in those days when story books were few, and good people's thoughts restrictive and austere."

"Well, husband," said Mrs. Oldham, "though one should be glad the prejudice against fiction as such no longer prevails, yet it seems to me children are nowadays exposed to very great perils of another sort, against which there are not so many kindly providences and protections. You would not like our children to have free range through the fictitious literature of the age?"

"By no means, my dear—certainly not while their taste and principles were unformed. Even if there were no bad books to be avoided, I should be sorry to have them lose the proper cultivating effect of works of true creative genius, by forgetting that 'half is bigger than the whole,' as old Hesiod says.

"Phil, my dear, may be safely left to himself. He never reads for mere story. His good taste is as unerring as instinct; I have been surprised to notice how it leads him to avoid every thing that is not either of the choicest quality, or else for some reason necessary to be read by every man of liberal culture.

"But as to Lilly and Fred, they devour books

for the mere pleasurable excitement of story, adventure, or incident. We must look well after them, not only to keep them from books that are bad, but from too many that are good."

The curious reader, impatient to know more about the Doctor, may think this chapter and the last one, a great breach of good faith and of the promise made two chapters before.

But, in the first place, let him consider the reservation with which the promise was made. Then let him read the next chapter, and he will see that he is indebted to these for the information he will find in that. For it led the Doctor on to speak of himself, and what he said gave me something to relate of his personal life before I knew him.

CHAPTER X.

GLIMPSES BIOGRAPHICAL AND AUTO-BIOGRAPHICAL — WITH OBSERVATIONS INTERSPERSED THAT ARE WORTH A CHAPTER IN THEMSELVES.

"There can be no greater blessing," continued the Doctor, after musing for a while, "than to be born in the light and air of a cheerful, loving home. It not only ensures a happy childhood—if there be health and a good constitution—but it almost makes sure a virtuous and happy manhood, and a fresh young heart in old age. I think it every parent's duty to try to make their children's childhood full of love and of childhood's proper joyousness; and I never see children destitute of them through the poverty, faulty tempers, or wrong notions of their parents, without a heartache. Not that all the appliances which wealth can buy are necessary to the free and happy unfolding of childhood in body, mind, or heart—quite otherwise, God be thanked; but children must at least have love inside the house, and fresh air and good play and some good companionship outside—otherwise young life runs the greatest danger in the world of withering or growing stunted, or sour and wrong, or at best prematurely old and turned inward on itself.

"My childhood was healthy and happy—a free and joyous beginning of life, with plenty of love and good books inside the house, and plenty of fresh air and good play outside, with boys and dogs, and ponies and kites, and hoops and footballs, and skates and sleds. All these blessings, I thank God"—said the Doctor, reverently looking upward—"were mine in abundance."

I saw the Doctor's thoughts were going back over the past; so I ventured an inquiry about his father, thinking he might be in a communicative mood. He was so, and went on.

"My father (for whom our oldest boy, Philip, is named) came to this country from England near the beginning of the present century, and settled in the city of Boston, where he devoted himself first to the study, and afterwards to the practice of the law. After a few years he married a Boston woman, the daughter of a distinguished member of the bar, as admirable for her domestic virtues as for the charms of her person and mind. Following his English tastes, he fixed his home in a pleasant villa at Brookline, a little way out of town, but near enough for convenient access to his office. There I was born, in the last year of the administration of Thomas Jefferson.

"I consider my father to have been one of the happiest and most fortunate of men. He thought so himself. He had his own notions of the conditions of a happy life; and they were all combined in his case. He had, first, uniform good health—the sort of good health and the spirits attending it, which result from a good constitution and good habits, particularly abundant exercise in the open air, mostly on horseback, in which sort of exercise he took great pleasure. Then again, he had something to do which he liked to do: he liked his profession—for the play of his faculties it demanded and gave scope to, and for the connection into which it brought him with the eminent men of his own degree. He was in the next place, free from ambition, avarice and envy—and blest with a competence that left him without a care. And finally, to crown all, his life was rounded with love: he was married to the woman he loved, fitly mated with one who was to him a most true and loving wife ; they had loving children, dear to them both ; and a happy home, where no cloud of peevishness or ill-humor ever darkened the sunshine.

"My father came to this country with strong democratic notions, imbibed from his intercourse with Robert Southey, with whom he formed a friendship at Oxford that lasted through life. There he came also to share his friend's scruples about subscription to the articles, which involved the loss of a rich ecclesiastical living in the gift of the family, that had been destined for him, and put him upon the necessity of turning to some other career, and probably, in connection with his political predilections (so much at variance with the good old Church and State sentiments of his family), inspired him with the idea of coming to this country.

"Time, and observation of the practical working of our institutions, disenchanted him of whatever was fantastic and extravagant in the opinions he had formed—yet without the reaction carrying him quite so far in the opposite direction as his friend Southey went. He came to see quite clearly that there is no charm or magic virtue in a mere form of government ;—that the form is nothing in itself ;— that the best government is that which is best fitted for the people ;—that of free governments the English is best for the English, and ours for us—provided it shall turn out there is wisdom and virtue enough in our people to make it the best. All which are the veriest common-places of sensible opinion nowadays, but which it needed a sensible man to arrive at gradually at that time, if in the fervor of generous youth, through hatred of despotism and oppression, he had been led to adopt such notions of popular rights, democratic institutions, and social regeneration, as my father had imbibed.

"In my seventeenth year, my father, who had twice before visited England alone, took my mother and the children with him, to see their relatives there. His father, the Dean, was delighted to see us all; and my father's conversion from what the good Dean naturally regarded as the deplorable errors of his early notions on religion and government, gave him unbounded satisfaction.

"My father's grandfather, Sir Oldham Oldham, of Oldham Hall, a Baronet of very ancient family, had gone to his forefathers with undiminished faith in the intimate and indissoluble relation between the existence of the universe and the house of Oldham—a faith that had been reverently handed down from a remote Saxon ancestry. But luckily for the universe, and particularly for that part of it within his orbit, it was also a point of honor with him to look upon his position and wealth as dignities and trusts to be upheld and discharged, rather than as mere personal possessions; so he took all possible care and pains to be, and in point of fact was (not, however, without much formal amplitude of speech and procedure) an upright and useful magistrate and a good landlord, and was in turn much respected by his country neighbors, and looked up to with profound reverence and affection by the numerous tenants and laborers within his broad manorial bounds.

"The vicarage of Oldham, which my father's scruples had made it impossible for him to take, had been given to a cousin of his. For more than three hundred years it had been as much a matter of course to see an Oldham at the Vicarage as at the Hall. That was the family way of making it all right about the great tithes. What if these went to the Hall? The Hall gave the parish an Oldham for vicar. Was not that better than a parson sent to them by some Lord Chancellor, or other remote patron? So from generation to generation some younger son of the house of Oldham had been duly sent to Oxford, and duly brought back to the incumbency of Oldham vicarage—which, in spite of the impropriation of the tithes, was still a very ample and dignified living. My grandfather the Dean had held it, and it had been destined (as I have said) for my father, as soon as he should have finished his Oxford studies. My father's turn of mind which prevented his taking it was a sore disappointment to his father and grandfather, and a mortification to all the Oldhams: it had never entered into the mind of any of them to conceive the like before. But this soreness was all over now; and we found ourselves welcome guests everywhere—at Christ Church, at the Vicarage, and at Oldham Hall, where my father's uncle, a new Sir Oldham Oldham, had succeeded to the dignities and duties of the head of the house.

"When the time came for returning home, my grandfather prevailed to have me left behind to finish my studies at Oxford under his particular direction; so I remained for four happy years within the walls of old Christ Church. The good old man was full of kindness, and if he could have had his way, would have kept me in England, believing there was no academical, ecclesiastical, or civil dignity, to which with my abilities (as he was pleased to say), and the family influence, I might not aspire. But my heart bid me back to my native land, and to the happy home of my childhood—to which I returned, glad to find all well there, and glad to be gladly welcomed back."

The Doctor paused, and fell into a musing mood, which lasted for some time—his thoughts, as I fancied, running along over his life since those youthful days. At length he broke silence:

"How worse than empty is a life of selfish struggle! To be born to an eminent place, with great work to do—that is something which those whose faculties fit them for the place and work may perhaps thank God for, though it has its great temptations. To be carried upward into the high places of the earth and invested with its distinctions and honors, without a selfish seeking for them, but merely in the sequel and result of brave and noble doing of the duty put upon us by God and man—like Washington—is something to be accepted with magnanimity, or enjoyed with modest satisfaction, according to one's temperament and tastes. To seek even a noble and lofty sphere of public action at the prompting of a great and energetic nature, conscious of abilities to render good service to one's country or to mankind and of the impulse to do so—this is something I shall not disparage or contemn. But a life of mere self-seeking vanity and pride—engendering envy, ill will, and all evil passions—wretched if success crown not its selfish struggles, and not made blessed by any success—what a miserable thing it is! What is life worth without inward peace? Which no selfish life can give."

"But you have no life of selfish struggles, successful or unsuccessful, to look back over," said I.

"I thank God, no," replied the Doctor; "if I have aspired to but little and done but little, I have no disappointed ambitions to embitter the recollections of the past."

CHAPTER XI.

HOW NATURE SHOWS HER GLADNESS.—JUNE AND JUNEFULNESS.—WHEN A NOSE IS A GOOD THING.—IS IT AN ORGAN FOR THE BEAUTIFUL. — THE GLORIES OF OCTOBER. — NATURE'S PICTURE GALLERY.—ART AND ITS LIMITATIONS.—MRS. OLDHAM ASKS TWO VERY GREAT QUESTIONS.

Mrs. OLDHAM had been away for ten days, on a visit to her mother. The Doctor had been quite dull and stupid for the last two or three days; but his mopishness vanished with his wife's return. She came back towards evening, just at the moment when one of those wonderfully gorgeous and beautiful sunset scenes was kindling up, which we have so often up here, particularly at this season of the year.

"See," said the Doctor, leading his wife to the west window of the library, "how glad nature is to have you back again. Not that we are not all as glad as nature is; but we cannot express it in such a rich grand way. See, the hills and the sky across the river are all aglow with many-hued blushes of delight—blue, gold, orange-colored and purple gleams of joy mantling the old rugged weather-beaten faces of the hills!"

"Nature is very obliging, as well as you," said Mrs. Oldham; "she is very apt to conform her expression to the mood of feeling with which one looks at her. But that is a glorious sight."

The next forenoon we were standing—Mrs. Oldham, the Doctor, and myself—in the veranda that shades the west end of the library, and which is built around it in a corresponding semi-octagonal shape. It was one of the finest of October days. The Doctor's spirits were as brisk as a bobolink.

"Mrs. Oldham," said he, "how bright and calmly joyous nature is. What a mild satisfaction rests on her countenance. You can see it through the thin haze veil she has thrown over her face to soften the light of the cloudless sun. It is all along of your return."

"What a beautiful month October is," said she.

"Yes," replied the Doctor, "no month in the year, on the whole, is more agreeable to me than October mostly is in this part of the world. It has not the special charm of May—the delicious feeling of soft, genial airs, after the sharp winds of March and the miserable chills that sometimes go through your bones and marrow in April. It is unlike June, when June is what it should be, with its ineffable, incomparable *Junefulness*—the blending of the rich green of its grass and foliage with its bloom and fragrance—a fragrance which makes a nose a good thing to have in the country (as Mr. Sparrowgrass might say), however undesirable it is in the city, a fragrance which almost elevates the nose into an organ for the beautiful.

"Noticeable, by the way," continued the Doctor, going off at a tangent on a new line of thought—a thing not unusual with him, and one you may always expect when you see him throw back his head and put his left hand to the back of his neck, and peer through his glasses at nothing in particular—"noticeable," said he, "that we should have no right to speak of a beautiful fragrance, any more than of a beautiful flavor—a soup or a sauce; that there is strictly nothing beautiful in the world of sense but what is so for the eye or for the ear—that forms, or colors, or tones, or words, are, in some combination or other, the elements of every sensible object that we rightly term beautiful, the only materials the creative power of the artist can employ to embody and express to the universal mind and heart the invisible and ineffable ideal, the beautiful in spirit and in truth.

"My friend Pelham tells me of an acquaintance of his, an eminent musical man, who denies this, who says that the fragrance of the heliotrope expresses to him precisely what certain musical tones do. He is the only man I ever heard of holding any such notion; and his experience, taking it as he states it, proves nothing to any purpose against the general doctrine. Yet I do not wonder at any one feeling reluctant to put the fragrance of flowers into the class of mere sensual delights. We do not feel so in regard to flavors. The delight of Alderman Gubbins in the turtle soup he gobbles down and in the champagne he follows it with, we know and admit is but a swinish delight—whether he call his turtle and champagne beautiful or delicious; but when the gentle Amanda puts the sprig of heliotrope, or mignionette, or the bunch of carnations to her nose and cries 'Beautiful!' dare you call it a swinish delight? do you even like to say, it is a mere delight of the senses, highly refined indeed in its quality, but still something purely and wholly sensual?

"Yet, granting (as we must) that the fragrance of a flower is no part of its beauty, one thing is certain, that, for me at least, no flower without fragrance is satisfactory, whatever be its beauty of form and color. I should as soon think of being satisfied with the lovely Amanda—her perfect form, her exquisite beauty of features and complexion—if she were made of painted wax or plaster. What the coursing life, what the soul is to Amanda, that the sweet fragrance is to a beautiful flower. When I am abroad in June, the thousand blended perfumes which the flowers exhale, seem to me not only the breath, but the soul of nature's life; and I almost feel as if I belonged to the world of beauty as much in virtue of my nose as of my eyes."

"But what were we talking about," said the Doctor, recollecting himself enough to be conscious he had wandered, but not enough to remember from where.

"*You* were beginning to sing the praises of October," replied Mrs. Oldham, with a smile, "and were contrasting it with June."

"Oh! ah! yes!" said the Doctor, "October is not like June; but it is delightful in the contrast of its genial temperature, its fresh, dry, invigorating air, with the burning sun of midsummer and the unelastic enervating atmosphere of dog-days. You can walk briskly without getting uncomfortably heated, or you can saunter about at the slowest pace without any sense of chill.

"But the great glory of October up here is in the face that nature wears—its day skies and sunset skies, but especially its forests and wooded hills.

"Can any thing be more exquisite than the scene that presents itself to our eyes now—both in near and in the distant view, in their union and in their contrast. This little valley widening out toward the river and forming our lawn, which we have dotted here and there with evergreens and flowering shrubs; and that brook, winding through the close-shaven and still green grass, gurgling and sparkling as its stream breaks over the stones, and running rapidly away to the place where it leaps down the rocks in the cascade that Phil has made the most of. By the way, Phil has shown the skill of an engineer, as well as the good taste of a landscape artist, in the way he has managed to enlarge that brook, by liberating the spring at the foot of the crag in the rear of the house, and to conduct the augmented stream through the garden and the lawn. That brook is a charming feature in the foreground of the picture before us. Then on the sides of the crags that flank our happy valley, see the leaves of the wild vines that grow out of the fissures all turned orange and red in contrast with the green of the tiny cedars they run among and twine around. And then, farther away to the south, over those fields and woods this side the reach in the river, and across the river to the west, see the myriad hues of the forest trees. Can any thing be more rich and gorgeously beautiful! To be up here, on such a day as this, on the hills and among the hills, and in the presence of higher hills and mountains, like those across the river, doubling and trebling their outlines as they recede in the distance in the cloudless sky, with the great sky lines of the Shawangunk and Catskills there on the farthest range of the horizon—it is positively glorious! See, too, what a soft blue haze invests every thing in the distance—the fields and woodlands and hills, and especially in the horizon where the land and the sky meet. It makes one think that nature is doing as a beautiful woman, when, at the prompting of the sweet instincts of womanhood, she drops her veil before her face in modest self-respect and rebuke of your too admiring gaze: or, since this soft haze is too thin a veil to do more than heighten the charms which it seems to conceal, it may be that nature lets fall the thin blue veil only the more to draw and fix our gaze."

"Ah, husband," said Mrs. Oldham, "that's a bad fancy, that last image of yours. You should think of nature as too natural to practise coquettish arts."

"Well, wife," replied the Doctor, "she is at any rate full of graces beyond the reach of art. Pencils of Claude and Ruysdael! How much of beauty does one see on such a day as this which no painter can portray—the fluctuations of light and shade, and the perpetual stir and motion of the life of nature; and even of the picturable things which the artist can fix and reproduce, what a series it would make—enough to fill a moderate cabinet—if we had a copy of all the different beautiful scenes our eyes can take in from this single point."

"I wish we had," said Mrs. Oldham, "I should be delighted to have such a set of paintings: for although the pictures nature hangs out for us in this grand gallery are so beautiful, and although so much of this beauty—changing with the changing seasons of the year, and shifting with the shifting lights and shades of every day is—unpicturable;

still, does not the true artist, even in copying, heighten the beauty of such scenes?"

"Is it," replied the Doctor, "any heightening—any thing the artist *adds* to the beauty of the scene? Is it not merely the peculiar pleasure you feel in seeing what nature gives you out-doors on such a large scale, copied and reduced to miniature by the artist? The original is beautiful, and so the copy must be too. The beauty the same in both, the same must be the pleasure—so far as due to the beauty. Can there be any difference except in the special pleasure of tracing the likeness of the copy to the original?"

"I suppose not," said Mrs. Oldham, "that is, I suppose there can be nothing more in regard to any mere copy. But you do not mean to deny that the artist may not only heighten the beauty of nature, but make things that will be more beautiful than any thing that can be actually found in nature?"

"No," answered the Doctor, "there is an ideal in the mind which surpasses any thing actual; and so nature and art both suggest more than they display—reveal to the mind's eye more than is visible to the eye of sense—disclose the ideal in the real, the infinite in the finite. The artist is a maker,

His faculty is creative. So he can and often does heighten the actual beauty of nature. It is too the necessity of his genius that he should strive to make things more beautiful than any thing that can be found in actual nature. But I would not say that his creations must needs be so, to be true works of art: yet certainly his function is to make things that have no exact counterpart in nature. Otherwise his faculty is not creative; he is not a true maker. But the creative imagination can work only with materials furnished by nature, with images derived from sense either directly or through the fancy. The maker, the finite maker at least—whether poet, or painter, or sculptor, or musician—cannot create out of nothing. He must have sensible means—words, colors, forms, tones—to embody and express his thought. By the way, it is curious that the word poet—which means only a maker—should have come to be exclusively appropriated to the maker of word creations. All artists are makers too, and eminently such. Yet there was a time in which the word maker in our Saxon speech was used instead of the word poet, and was applied to word artists in the same exclusive or eminent way as the term poet is now. It seems to indicate a general feeling, as if word poetry were the highest order of artistic creation."

"It seems to me," said Mrs. Oldham, "unnecessary and something invidious thus to put into comparison things that are different, rather than of unequal rank. But as to that Beautiful in itself, which is embodied in the finite maker's forms—what is it?"

"What else is it"—said the Doctor in reply—"what else can it be, but the reflection, more or less faint but always faint, of the infinite in the finite? What is all Art but an attempt at the impossible? No sum of finites can equal the infinite. The Almighty artist himself needs eternity and immensity to disclose the riches of His mind and thought. When will the disclosure be complete? When will the Infinite pass fully out into the finite? Eternally unfolding, but eternally undisclosed, is the infinite substance and source of Truth, Beauty and Goodness."

"Husband," said Mrs. Oldham, "when did creation begin, and what was God's purpose in it?"

"We will ask Professor Clare about it some time," replied the Doctor.

CHAPTER XII.

PROFESSOR CLARE.—THE DOCTOR'S TALK ABOUT THE STARRY HEAVENS.—ADDISON AND SHAKSPEARE.—WORD-PAINTING AND OTHER PAINTING.—WHERE THE UNIVERSE ENDS AND HOW IT IS FILLED.—MRS. OLDHAM'S TWO QUESTIONS ARE NOT ANSWERED.

PROFESSOR CLARE came in that evening to tea. He is the Doctor's neighbor, an alert little man with curly black hair and bright eyes, who, besides knowing Greek (his special profession), knows pretty nearly every thing else that is going on in the neighborhood, and in the world at large, for that matter, so far as a daily reading of the New York *Daily Times* can keep a man up with the times. He is a fluent utterer of the current common-places of opinion and sentiment upon all such things as are made matters of opinion and sentiment in his world and among those he has mostly lived with; and also thinks he has a thought or two upon profounder matters of theology and philosophy gained many years ago—during his last year at college in fact, where he went in succession through Locke, Edwards and Paley, Reid, Stewart, and Butler, making daily recitations out of them to the President, the Reverend Doctor Dort, but without getting much clear insight into the differences that divide those celebrated writers—owing, perhaps, to the fact that the venerable President appeared to hold all those authors as thinkers of equal and harmonious authority, requiring of the students a respectful recollection of their words, rather than encouraging any perplexing inquiries about their meaning and agreement with each other. Venerable Doctor Dort ! He slept well through life ; and has slept peacefully in the resting-place where his reverend head has reposed for nearly thirty years, in the cemetery of W—— College—where (not in the cemetery, but in the college) Mr. Clare afterwards for some years held the professorship of Greek— cherishing a filial reverence for the venerable slumberer as the "guide, philosopher, and friend," through whose guidance, philosophy, and friendship, he explored the deepest regions of the world of thought, and brought back specimens and mementoes which he sometimes takes pleasure (like most travellers) in showing to his friends.

But Greek was his profession; and Greek is his great love—a love that betrays itself at times in mixed society, at dinner and tea parties, where he is a little given to favoring the company with illustrations of whatever may be the topic of conversation drawn from those old sources, the sayings of famous Greek writers or the doings of famous Greek great men. But then he is such a thoroughly amiable good-natured man, and so full of pleasant chat that everybody likes him, and his absence from the tea-parties would be felt as a great loss.

"Friendly persons," the Doctor says, speaking of him, "always make friends, certainly among all right-hearted people; and as to the rest, we all have our little foibles, as the Frenchman said when ETC.; and for my part, I think I like a friendly-hearted man the better for having a foible or two —provided, of course, that they imply no meanness, nothing dishonorable, but rather spring from warmth of heart, simplicity, confiding frankness, and an unaffected love for some respectable or harmless hobby."

The ETCETERA above refers (I may observe by the way) to the Frenchman's particular foible—a remarkable taste in the matter of *bouilli*—which cannot be considered either as respectable or harmless, and which I abstain from mentioning in full because I do not like to present an image to the fancy that might possibly be unpleasing to some of my gentle readers. Some things may as well be left unsaid, even when it is not possible to avoid suggesting them. But in this case I have suggested nothing to those who have not heard of the Frenchman's little foible. Those that have, must not blame me (if the image be in any degree unpleasing to their taste), but the Doctor, and scarcely even him, but only the ill-luck that first brought the image before their fancy. The Doctor, however, is not squeamish about such matters. He likes to refer to this saying of the Frenchman, and often does so, always giving the *etcetera* in full—beause it gives piquancy to the common-place and so justifies its utterance.

But Professor Clare and the Frenchman's foible have led me away from the purpose of the chapter—which was to record the talk that fell out this evening—and to this I must return.

Tea was served (as it always is) in the library, at a little table near the bay-window. We sat looking out upon the golden sunset, and the gorgeous hues of the horizon on the tops of the hills across the Hudson, until the last gleam of daylight and twilight faded away. But it would not be true to say, as in Coleridge's lackadaisical (wilfully lackadaisical) sonnet, that "Eve saddened into Night." For the night was any thing but sad. The sky was cloudless, and the air was just in the right state to give the stars the brightest possible twinkle, as they came out one after another. We stepped out upon the lawn to get a larger view of the brilliant sight. The whole concave, from horizon to welkin, was studded with glittering lights.

"What a sight," said the Doctor—"so glorious, yet so still! How silently they shine."

"Not without voice, though," replied the Professor.

> "What though in solemn silence all
> Move round this dark terrestrial ball,
> What though no real voice nor sound,
> Amid those radiant orbs be found,
> In reason's ear they all rejoice,
> And utter forth a glorious voice—
> Forever singing as they shine:
> The Hand that made us is Divine."

"That's grand, isn't it? That's the old Greek idea of the music of the spheres—the divine harmony of Pythagoras."

"Hardly that," said the Doctor, "since it is far from clear that the Pythagorean music of the spheres—which was a mathematical harmony of numbers—had any thing but an impersonal principle for the ultimate law of the universe, or rather for the ground out of which it was evolved in a purely necessary way: which would not be a very orthodox idea of God according to Addison's view of the matter. Still there is no doubt but this idea of the music of the spheres, which comes from the harmony of the heavenly motions, is very old; and it is as poetic and beautiful as it is old.

"But who has expressed it like Shakspeare in that moonlight scene in the Merchant of Venice:

> . . . . . "Look how the floor of heaven
> Is thick inlaid with patines of bright gold;
> There's not the smallest star which thou behold'st,
> But in his motion like an angel sings,
> Still quiring to the young ey'd cherubins:
> Such harmony is in immortal souls;
> But, whilst this muddy vesture of decay
> Doth grossly close it in, we cannot hear it."

"That's finer than your verses, grand as they are."

"Why, I recollect now," said the Professor, "that Doctor Vox, in his celebrated lecture on the

Cavalier, introduced both those passages, and praised the latter as the finest."

"Yes," replied the Doctor, "I recited them to him one day as we were speaking of something that led me to think of them and put them in contrast. 'Grand!' said Doctor Vox. 'I'll bring them into my lecture on the *Cavalier.*' I heard him repeat his lecture afterwards, and found he had brought them in. Their logical connection with his subject was not remarkably strict, but they were delivered with an air, and made a good rhetorical point that told well.

"But what exquisite grace, what simple idiomatic perfection of language, in that passage of Shakspare's! What a picture it presents to the mind's eye; and what a proof of the superiority of word pictures over form and color pictures, or rather, I ought to say, of the wider reach and greater variety of the power of words for the expression of the conceptions which the poetic imagination gives form to: yet the secret of their power in the use of them is ever in using them as Shakspeare does—not as something fine in themselves, but merely as instruments of expression, and the simpler the better, so they be fitly chosen,— and who chooses them like Shakspeare? Words!

Wonderful things are words—half spirit, half sense, so flexible, so various in their power! The poet can body forth to the fancy or to the imaginative faculty in words almost every thing the sculptor or the painter can in form and color, and a great deal that form and color cannot embody. What painter could give adequate form to the picture that Shakspeare in these words puts before the mind's eye."

"But sculpture and painting can sometimes do more than poetry can do," said the Professor; "they can give us at a glance, vividly and perfectly, many things which words can only imperfectly express, and that not merely delicate varieties of outline and light and shade, but also thereby of moral expression, for instance, of a countenance."

"True," replied the Doctor, "and it is another advantage of sculpture and painting (as also of music) that they are, as my friend Weir says, more catholic arts, in one point of view—their *language* is universal; they not only speak to the mind and heart of humanity everywhere in the matter of what they speak (which all art does), but their language is one that is read and understood alike by the people of all different nations and tongues.

"Still the proper effect of true art is rather to suggest the ideal to the mind's eye, than to reproduce the actual to the eye of sense; and besides, the poet, in embodying his conceptions of action or passion, thought or sentiment, is not limited like the painter and sculptor, to some fixed point in space and to some indivisible moment of time: and so I speak of poetry as having a wider reach and greater variety of power than the other arts. But I intend nothing invidious. All the arts are alike in their object, the expression of the beautiful; they are heterogeneous in their means of expression, and so in some respects cannot be justly put into comparison: *heterogenea non sunt comparanda;* a lily cannot be said to be whiter than a rose is sweet. I am sure, however, you will agree with me in saying that no painter can paint the picture which those words of Shakspeare paint for the mind's eye. The listening cherubs—form and color might picture them; but that would be far from telling the whole story."

"I think you are right," said the Professor.

Mrs. Oldham had remained behind a moment or two when we came out. She is liable to neuralgia, and was afraid to be out, even on such a dry warm evening as this, without her hood and shawl:

so she had stopped to get them ; and in her womanly carefulness had brought along also the gentlemen's hats. She now interposed :

"O you men," said she, "talking abstract talk about pictures with such pictures before you as the sky presents ! If you must speculate, let it be about the stars. Think of them—such a multitude of worlds."

"There are as many on the other side of the equator," said the Doctor, "which we never see ; and the dwellers on that side never see ours ; and from both us and them the sun hides more by day than the night reveals."

"Then to think of them," said Mrs. Oldham, "as such great worlds hanging on nothing, and moving about in such vast circles—so far from us that the light (though moving at the rate of nearly two hundred thousand miles a second) takes nearly three years to get to us from the nearest fixed star ! I was reading about it to-day."

"Where is that star ?" asked the Professor.

"There it is," said the Doctor, pointing to it. "It is the brightest of those stars in the constellation called *Centaur*. And look, there is another star of the first magnitude—in the constellation *Lyra*—that very bright star ; it is called Vega, and is so far off that it takes twelve years for a ray of light from it to reach our eyes."

"And how far would that make it from us?" asked Mrs. Oldham.

"More than seventy billions of miles," replied the Doctor. "But the light from a star of the sixth magnitude is ninety-six years in coming to us, and is nearly six hundred billions of miles distant; and from a star of the twelfth magnitude (seen only by a telescope), the light is four thousand years on its way to us, and has to travel twenty-four thousand billion miles."

"And beyond that you suppose still other worlds which no telescope can reach—don't you?" asked Mrs. Oldham.

"Yes, a billion billion miles beyond the farthest star which we behold, there are doubtless other worlds and systems—and so outward and outward —worlds upon worlds, systems upon systems."

"Husband, where does the universe end?"

"Nowhere, my dear."

"Is infinitude filled?"

"Yes and no."

"Why yes?"

"We cannot but think of that which we behold as a part and a type of that which exists in the infinite abyss beyond our view."

" Why no ? "

" Because the infinite is infinite, and no sum of finites can equal it."

" Are those worlds inhabited, do you think ? " asked the Professor.

" I have no doubt of it," replied the Doctor.

" I read a very profound and learned book," said the Professor, " that came out three or four years ago, going to prove the contrary, or, at least, that there is no good reason for the common faith."

" And it proved neither the one nor the other," said the Doctor ; " all it proved was—what everybody knew before—that the dwellers in those heavenly bodies must be differently constituted from those that live on our earth in order to exist there : and so, because there can be no human dwellers there, the author inferred that there are none at all —an irresistible inference, indeed, provided it be taken for granted that God could not make living and rational creatures adapted to those worlds as easily as he has done so here ; which is a principle the writer does not prove and which I do not grant, so his argument goes for nothing with me : and on the other hand, the fact that God has filled our earth so full of various forms of life adapted to such opposite conditions, is a presumption he has done the like in the other worlds. It is repugnant to my mind to suppose that our little globe is the only abode of reasonable beings; I the rather belive that the countless myriads of orbs that roll in the boundless depths of space, are full of dwellers of like order and many probably of higher degree than those that inhabit our earth."

"And to think, husband, that He who made all those worlds and filled them with dwellers, should watch over and care for each individual of us all, with that constant special care He bids us believe He does."

"Costs Him nothing, my dear; it is as easy as if the universe were a twenty acre lot, and you and I the only children of His care."

"But why suppose such minute individual care?" said Professor Clare.

"Because," replied the Doctor, "it is best to consider God as at least equally as good as a good earthly father."

"Let us go in," said Mrs. Oldham.

CHAPTER XIII.

MORE ABOUT THE STARS AND THE EARTH—PANTHEISM—WHETHER ANY THING CAN BECOME SO SMALL AS TO BECOME NOTHING AND YET REMAIN SOMETHING—TIME AND SPACE—MRS. OLDHAM'S TWO GREAT QUESTIONS AGAIN, AND THE WAY THEY WERE ANSWERED.

"Here is that little book about 'the Stars and the Earth,' which I was reading to-day," said Mrs. Oldham, as we drew around the library-table; "there are a great many beautiful and wonderful things in it about the distance of the stars, and the time the light takes to come from them to our eyes: but there are some speculations about time and space that seemed to me very strange, and far from true. But I don't think I understood the reasoning at all."

"No matter, my dear, about what you did not understand," replied the Doctor; "you understood all that was much worth your understanding—those facts about the stars and light; and as to the speculations, your impressions were quite correct. Have you read it, Professor?"

The Professor had never seen it.

"It contains some novel and striking, some ingenious and beautiful things," continued the Doctor, "but it is full of absurd confusions of thought, and of false assumptions grounded on them—leading to the strangest contradictions. The writer regards the universe as God's thought—a beautiful idea, and rightly taken, true enough."

"But it is Pantheism, is it not?" said Professor Clare.

"What is Pantheism?" asked the Doctor.

"Well, it is every thing God and God every thing," was the Professor's reply.

"Both at once, do you mean, Professor?"

The Professor confessed he did not see any difference.

"Well, you are not the only one that does not: but we will not go into that now," said the Doctor; "I had rather ask you in what way that expression about the universe being God's thought strikes you as Pantheistic?"

"Why, it makes the universe exist *in* God," answered the Professor.

"In Him we live and move and have our being—saith St. Paul," rejoined the Doctor.

The Professor looked puzzled.

"How do you mean?" said he.

"Nothing," returned the Doctor, "except that you should not press upon figurative or ambiguous expressions a bad construction, simply because it is possible. St. Paul was no Pantheist, yet you might in that way easily make him out one."

By the way, this remark of the Doctor's strikes upon a vice, which I, the Doctor's editor, cannot help here remarking upon. It is the vice of a great many persons, especially of bigoted religious people with only a certain degree of education—half instructed preachers—who hold a certain number of accredited formulas without any insight—who do not think, but only think they think, and are particularly mistaken in thinking they are philosophical thinkers. Such persons are very prone to raise an outcry against any thing that jars with their habitual notions, and to put the worst construction upon every thing that is not expressed after the fashion of their formulas.

There is almost no amount of absurd mistake, or moral enormity of unjust censure which bigotry and prejudice, combined with ignorance or insufficient instruction, may not commit. It is wonderful and pitiful there should be, in the highest ecclesiastical quarters, such a degree not only of the bigotry you might expect, but of the ignorance you would not expect. I recollect the case of a passage out of John Calvin's Institutes being denounced as rank popery, by one of the chief doctors at the oldest fountain head of the theological instruction of one of the great religious communions that claims John Calvin as its founder and guide, and the persons who had reprinted an old tractate in which that passage occurred (but without reference, and so the source of it was not indicated), were held up to the odium of all the old women in the land! If the chief shepherds of the people—the teachers of the teachers—can do this, how will it be with the under teachers and the people they teach!

But Professor Clare was not a bigot, and the Doctor had no thought of intimating he was. But to go on with the talk.

"You are right, as well as not right, in what you observed," continued the Doctor. "It is possible to construe the expression about the universe being God's thought, so as to imply the immanence of all things in God,—either as a mode of God's being—taking God as an infinite, impersonal substance, or as a mode of His activity—making Him the only personal being; the former destroying

God's personality, the latter ours, and both of them incompatible with the idea of any proper moral government. But it is not necessary to construe the expression in that way; it may regard the universe as God's productive thought, the projection of His activity, distinct and separate from Himself, just as the artist's picture is; which I take to be this writer's idea, and so not implying any thing wrong in his way of thinking about God. And as to the rest, the spirit of his little book is thoroughly religious—its whole purpose being (as he says) to help us 'imagine and completely understand the universe to be the work of a single Creator.'

"But the oddity of the thing is, that the author thinks the only possible way to do this is to show that 'a point of view is conceivable, from which the universe no longer requires the expansion of time and space in order to exist and to be intelligible to us'! And so he undertakes to establish this point of view, by denying the reality of time and space, or by proving that successions of events can take place in no time, and bodies can co-exist in no space! And his reasoning is equally odd. He takes an indefinitely small time or space to be the same as infinitely small, and both alike as equivalent to nothing."

"It seems to me he is right in that," said the Professor.

"The infinitely small is, no doubt, equivalent to nothing; but it is so only because there can be no such thing as an infinitely small thing—the idea is a contradiction: and as to the indefinitely small, though it may be regarded as nothing, it is not really so. If you set out with a given duration or a given space, you can conceive them indefinitely contracted—and so far as any practical or scientific operations are concerned, you may regard them as reduced to nothing; but you cannot conceive them as absolutely so reduced: it is a contradiction.—Is not this clear to you?"

"I cannot say it is," replied the Professor.

"Well, then," said the Doctor, "can you conceive a wheel to be so reduced in size as to become no wheel, and yet continue a wheel, and to increase the rapidity of its revolutions to such a degree as not to revolve at all, and yet keep going round?"

"Yes, that is supposable, so far as our eyes are concerned," replied the Professor; "photography and the microscope illustrate it."

"Completely, however," said the Doctor, "only

on the supposition that an exceedingly small thing is nothing. But things may become so small as to be nothing to our eyes, and yet be very far from being absolutely nothing. So you are partly right, partly not right, again. Photography contracts that pleasing picture of Queen Victoria's little girls into a space so small that our eyes can distinguish nothing, and our friend Doctor Pelham's microscope brings it back again distinct and clear. But that small point of space is still an expanse. Can photography make an image that would occupy no space? Can the microscope reveal such an image? In short, Professor, do you think it supposable that something can become nothing, and yet remain something?"

"Absolutely nothing and yet something?—no. I do not so opine," replied the Professor.

"You would not think, then, that because the actions of an hour can be hurried through in half an hour, therefore they can conceivably be hurried through in strictly no time?"

"I cannot so think."

"And you do not think that because my wife's fleecy shawl there can be compressed into a quarter of the space it now fills, it can conceivably be compressed into no space?"

"No."

"You do not, then, find yourself able to conceive that, because every finite duration and every finite space, when compared with infinite duration and infinite space, 'appears like nothing,' therefore they are strictly nothing?"

"I confess not."

"Would you say, then, that 'the proposition that for the occurrence of every given event, a certain lapse of time is requisite, may be altogether rejected'?"

"I would not."

"Then you would not, in like manner, reject the idea that some expansion of space is necessary for the existence and co-existence of bodies?"

"No."

"You would not, then, hold that the myriads of worlds we have seen to-night can be conceived as occupying in absolute reality no space at all, and the events of their history as transpiring in really no time at all?"

"I certainly cannot hold such a thing conceivable."

"And you would not consider such a conception as a wonderfully fine and wonderfully important one—as being 'the only one *with* which and *by* which we can imagine and completely understand the universe to be the work of a single Creator?'"

"By no means can I so consider it," replied the Professor.

"It is clear then," said the Doctor, "that you do not agree with the remarkable thinker who wrote this remarkable little book, for he holds all these droll notions."

"But how came he to fall into such notions? Does he go upon nothing that is true?" asked the Professor.

"Oh no," replied the Doctor, "that is never perhaps the case with any thinker. He only takes what is or may be true as to God, as true as to us."

"How do you mean?"

"God's knowledge may embrace all things in the universe—all things and events—at once without relation to Time and Space; and this writer tries to make it out that the same thing may be conceivably true of us—which could only be by our becoming infinite like God."

"What are Time and Space then?" inquired the Professor.

"The *where* of bodies and the *when* of events

to creatures like us," replied the Doctor, "necessary conditions of knowledge for finite minds—conceptions without which we cannot conceive of things and events."

"But, husband," interposed Mrs. Oldham, "there are my two questions that I put to you yesterday: you said you would ask Professor Clare about them: When did creation begin? and what was God's purpose in it? I want to hear about them."

"Well, my dear, they are rather deep questions both of them. What say you, Professor? The first one is rather the most puzzling, I imagine: When did creation begin?"

"Do you mean to ask when our earth was created?" said the Professor.

"No, I rather think my wife has not troubled herself with the questions raised by the geologists as to the duration of our earth: at any rate her question, I presume, has a wider range."

"Yes," said Mrs. Oldham, "I was thinking last night, as I was looking at the innumerable stars, how far back the first act of creation took place, and when the first created thing came into existence."

"It seems to me," said the Doctor, "there is a previous question: Did creation ever begin?"

"Certainly," answered the Professor, "we are sure it must have had a beginning, though we may be unable to say when—or how many ages back—that beginning was; for that is a matter of fact, to be learned only from competent instruction, and not of reasoning to be reached by our own thoughts."

"You mean," said the Doctor, "that as every thing that had a beginning must have had a cause, so every thing that had a cause must have had a beginning?"

"Yes," replied the Professor.

"But you would hold it conceivable that the universe did not come into existence all at once, but may have been the product of successive acts of the Creative Will?"

"I conceive it may so have been."

"And you would say, in regard to any particular determinate product of creative activity, that it must have come into existence at some particular determinate point or period in the eternity of duration?"

"I should say so."

"And you would consider that the very first act

of creative energy was prior, not only in the order of thought but in the order of time, to the existence of the first created thing?"

"I should so consider."

"And you would say there was a determinate time in the past when that very first act took place, and that first created thing began to exist?"

"I should so say."

"And how long had God then existed?" asked the Doctor again.

"From eternity, of course," replied the Professor.

"And from eternity, then, to that time, you conceive of God as doing nothing in the way of creation?" said the Doctor, continuing his questions.

"It seems necessary so to think," answered the Professor.

"From eternity to that time, you conceive of infinitude, then, as void, or filled by God alone?" said the Doctor.

"I must so conceive," said the Professor.

"From eternity, then, a solitary inactive God?" inquired the Doctor once more.

"Not necessarily solitary or inactive," replied the Professor; "there was the society and converse among themselves of the Persons of the Blessed Trinity."

"Humph!" said the Doctor, "if a God without a universe *from* eternity be a satisfactory conception, why not *to* eternity?"

"But, husband, when do *you* say creation began?" interposed Mrs. Oldham.

"When God began," replied the Doctor; "at least I should say so, if I had any doctrine to lay down on the matter, which I have not."

"But that would make creation eternal," said she.

"And that would be a contradiction," said the Professor.

"To the understanding, I know it is," returned the Doctor, "but it is more satisfactory to the reason than the idea of a God from eternity without a universe, and no more a contradiction to the understanding than the received doctrine about the eternal WORD by Whom all things were made. To be God, and to be ever creative, seem to me ideas that go inseparably together, though the former is first in the order of thought."

"But that would make creation necessary," suggested the Professor.

"Not in your sense of the word," returned the

Doctor; "no more so than God's own existence, and nature, and attributes as the Living God; no more so than the finite creations of the human artist, which are the product of his artist nature and faculties—in one view necessary, in another free. It is indeed necessary that God should be what He is. God is Love: the necessities of Love are the freest activities in the universe."

"But there's my other question," said Mrs. Oldham. "I want to hear Professor Clare's opinion about it: Why did God create the universe?"

"For His own glory," replied the Professor.

"Do you regard that as His final end?" inquired the Doctor.

"Yes," answered the Professor, "the display of His glory in the works of creation, and to the intelligent creatures whom He made capable of discerning it."

"Self-display, self-glorification is not regarded as a very respectable motive in finite rational creatures; and can it (with reverence) be considered an end worthy of God?" asked the Doctor.

"But I do not mean a selfish display: the manifestation works the happiness of the intelligent universe," said the Professor.

"Then the display is not the final end; but the

means to another end," said the Doctor. "But even the production of happiness is not the highest moral end conceivable."

"But do you exclude happiness?" said the Professor.

"No," replied the Doctor, "the Stoics were as wrong as the Epicureans. The Supreme Good is in the union of Goodness and Happiness—but the goodness is the higher end of the two."

"How do you regard the universe, then, in relation to God?" asked the Professor.

"As the work of an infinite artist, working out of Love. His creative work is indeed the reflection of Himself—revealing in countless myriads of finite forms His mind and heart—the highest product of His creative love being spiritual free creatures, the image of Himself, capable in their measure of conceiving in thought and of realizing in free will the ideas of Truth, Beauty and Goodness, of which He is the infinite substance and cause—a kingdom of which He is the Father and Lord, in which He dwells and over which He presides, that indwelling and providence being also a part of His artistic work. The universe is God's grand Drama, of which He is at once Poet and Manager;—Infinitude the theatre; Eternity the time of action; the Conflict of Good and Evil the secret of the plot and progress of the play; the Triumph of Good the final end :—a Drama eternally unfolding in His eye —the stage, the scenery, the situations all arranged, and the actors called forth in their turn and time by Him. The kingdom of Nature—all its creatures and powers are the unconscious and passive instruments of His will; but in the kingdom of Spirits, His creatures have the high function and sacred obligation of freely concurring with His design, and working for Him and with Him for the accomplishment of the final end. You and I and all spiritual creatures have our several parts, and to act well the part allotted to us, with a free and willing mind, is at once our dignity and our end, our goodness and our blessedness; and so only can we become participant of the Eternal Life of the Living God."

"But what if we do not, husband?"

"Well, my dear, it is not God's fault. He is always within us for light and for strength. As to the rest, it is never too late to repent."

CHAPTER XIV.

THE DOCTOR PREACHES TO HIS DAUGHTER—QUOTES WORDSWORTH AND GETS INTO HEROICS—ALSO HE FULFILS A SCRIPTURAL DUTY.—REMARKABLE STREET-SWEEPERS AND KNIFE-GRINDERS.—COMFORTING DOCTRINE CONCERNING SHIRT MAKING AND STOCKING MENDING.

LILLY OLDHAM is a great pet of her father's. I do not mean that her mother is not equally fond of her. She is so, but she does not show it in the same way. There is, I am apt to think, something in the quality of a father's love for a daughter, especially for an only daughter, that begets a peculiar tenderness of manner, a certain caressing playfulness, different from that which is prompted by a mother's love. Be this as it may, it is conceded, I believe, that fathers are apt to make pets of their daughters; and Lilly Oldham being an only daughter was not the less likely to be made one on that account.

She is a bright-eyed, bright-faced girl of fourteen, not regularly beautiful, but with a fine head, a noble forehead, clear dark eyes, a sweet smile, a joyous laugh, and a countenance full of expression —altogether more charming than any mere regular beauty; clear, keen, and quick as lightning in the play of her faculties, but impatient of long-continued application; generous and affectionate, impulsive and sensitive, but somewhat self-willed and inclined to amusement, and to indulgence of the mood and humor of the moment, rather than to profitable occupation, particularly in her reading. She gets indeed her school lessons faithfully and cheerfully enough; but as to the rest, finds much more pleasure in novels and tales, than in books of history and travels, or works of solid instruction. The height of felicity for her, when in the house, is to sit curled up in a heap on the sofa, with one of Scott's, or Dickens', or Kingsley's, or Miss Yonge's books on her knees, and her near-sighted eyes close to the page, reading aloud to her brother Fred. It makes no matter apparently to either of them how often the book has been read before. The enjoyment seems indeed to be fresher with every new reading of it.

Mrs. Oldham has always been aware of Lilly's faults, and has affectionately endeavored to correct them—not without success; for there is a visible improvement in her of late. But the Doctor, until lately, has thought of nothing but cultivating his children's qualities as playthings in his moments of leisure and relaxation—having perfect confidence in his wife's right guidance of them in all things else. He now rubs his eyes, and tries, he says, to realize that his little girl has grown so big as to need his care, but cannot rightly make it out. He admits, however, his duty, now that his wife has pointed it out to him, and tries to do it in the only way he can form any notion of—by preaching to her.

"Lilly, my dear child," said he one day to her, "we must all try to act upon principle and from a sense of duty."

"But, dear papa, don't you think it is dreadfully dreary, the way some persons talk about principle and duty? Don't you remember that divinity student to whom you said that the Good Lord was not so particular about some things as he was? He thought it very sinful for children to play in the garden on Sundays, even after they had been to church and had learned their catechism and hymns at home. You told him that if the children thought it was wrong, of course they ought not to do it, but that you thought Our Lord was just as much pleased to see them scamper about the garden walks after they had got their Sunday lessons, as He was when they were getting them—provided they had not been taught to think it wrong, and so could do it with a good conscience. He seemed to be very much shocked at what you said.

"Well, papa, I heard that same divinity student once say he always took his walks on principle, and laughed once a day from a sense of duty! It sounded so queer! I am sure you would not wish me to be like him,"—she added, coming up to his chair and leaning on his shoulder, and looking into his face with half laughing eyes,—"I walk because I enjoy it, and love to see the trees, and flowers, and hills, and the water and the sky; and as to laughing once a day from a sense of duty—it makes me laugh to think of such a thing! I laugh a hundred times a day because I cannot help it. Only think of that divinity student, going about with his face so solemn every day and all day long, except that one laugh from a sense of duty! It must be a dreadfully dreary laugh. I don't think I could join in it. It would frighten me just like the laugh of that stone image over the gate."

"Very well, Miss Moppet," said the Doctor, with a smile, smoothing back her soft dark brown hair and looking into her dancing eyes, "very well indeed, and cunningly put; but you must not escape me in this way. I have no objection to your laughing as often as you cannot help it. I like to see it and to hear it. There is nothing dreary in your laugh, nothing to frighten one like a laughing stone image; and I never knew you laugh when it was improper to do so.

"As to the rest, I allow full scope for all spontaneities and impulses, or—as I should say to you—for things that you do because you like to do them, or because you cannot help doing them.

"But, my dear little girl, life was not given us merely for scampering about among the birds and flowers, laughing and singing and dancing—with plenty of nice stories to read when we wish to sit still. There's your French and Algebra, and other school lessons to be learned: I don't say but you do them well enough. But there's your musical practice which you do not take to as kindly as you ought. Then there's your needle-work that your mother wants you to become expert in. And then there are a great many books of voyages and travels, and biography and history and poetry for you to read, which would be very pleasant to you if you would only once get well into them; as well as some other books not quite so entertaining perhaps, but which you must read if you would be an intelligent, well-informed woman.

"Now these things are duties for you. Yet you do not like them so well as some other things. I do not blame you for it. But what I want you to think of is, that it is just in regard to these things you must learn to live for duty rather than for inclination, to do what you ought to do rather than what you like best, if you would be either good or happy."

"But what a pity, dear papa, that duty and inclination should ever clash—that what I ought to do is not always what I want to do."

"That is, you are sorry, Lilly, that your duties will not always conform themselves to your inclinations?"

"How do you mean, papa?"

"I mean to ask whether you would bend your duties to your wishes, or your wishes to your duties?"

"Well, I suppose I was thinking what a pity it is that my duties would not be kind enough to stand aside, and let me have my way without staring me so sternly in the face all the time. That is not right, I know. But what a blessed thing if one's inclinations always went exactly along in the line of duty, without one's thinking any thing about it, or having to make any effort to go right."

"Ah, my child," said the Doctor, "that is an angelical (as we are wont to say) and not a human goodness. In childhood there is always innocence, and in some sweet-natured and saintly children there is a spontaneity of goodness that shows so like the angelical, that it makes one sad to think of the interval that lies between innocence and virtue,—and that emerging from innocence is not always a rising to virtue, and even if virtue do succeed to innocence, so much of the former sweet gracefulness is likely to be lost. But then we are to remember for our comfort, that mere innocent spontaneity, however right in its direction and sweet and beautiful in its manifestations, is not goodness, either angelical or human. Human goodness is in this world for the most part virtue,—a manly energy in doing our duty in spite of temptations to the contrary; and the harder the struggle—the stronger, that is, the temptations and the poorer the nature we received in respect of temper and disposition, appetites and passions—the greater the virtue if we do our duty. The good Lord has made us for virtue now, and so ordered our nature that virtue may in due time grow up and be unfolded, or transformed rather, into that angelical goodness in which reason and conscience, will and inclination will come to be at one, so that it will require no watchful care or painful effort to be good. Meantime we must be content that duty is our law, and self-denial for duty's sake our virtue, and we may be thankful it brings with it its own unspeakable reward of peace and well-being too."

"Duty," continued the Doctor, getting up into his unconscious "altitudes," as Phil called them; "Duty! O great word! O noble and beautiful thought! The faculty to think the thought, to speak the word, to feel its meaning and its power, attests our sublime destination. Duty! It is itself but a purely ideal conception—the idea of obligation to do right because it is right; yet purely ideal as it is in its essence, it is an idea which, when embodied and realized (as it may be) in men's purposes and actions, gives to human life and human history all its worth, all its nobleness—is the source of every thing most fair and beautiful and touching, of every thing great, heroic and sublime.

> 'Stern Lawgiver! yet thou dost wear
>   The Godhead's most benignant grace;
> Nor know we any thing so fair
>   As is the smile upon thy face:

> Flowers laugh before thee on their beds;
> And Fragrance in thy footing treads;
> Thou dost preserve the stars from wrong;
> And the most ancient Heavens, through thee, are fresh and strong.'

"But bless me," said the Doctor, suddenly recollecting himself, "how I have been running on—and out of your reach too, my dear little girl, is it not?"

"It is very beautiful, papa, and I think I understand a good deal of it. But that about the flowers and the stars is not so clear to me."

"Ah, my dear child, it means that it is nothing but obedience to the laws of their being that makes the flowers beautiful and fragrant, keeps the stars from getting out of place and the heavens from decaying through old age; and the poet gets very poetical about it, and speaks as if they were alive and knew those laws, and followed them of their own will. But the thing he intends to signify to us is that Duty is the Law of our Being and Well-Being, and we, who are above the flowers and the stars in knowing our law and in being able to follow it, must do of our own accord what they do blindly and of necessity—be obedient, that is, to God's will.

"The lines are from Wordsworth's grand Ode

to Duty, which you must learn, and I will talk to you about it some other time. But I will not go into any more heroics now. I only wanted to tell you that you must not be listless, nor spend your time in amusement, but must be busy to some good purpose.

"And what an example you have in your mother, my child. In the twenty years we have lived together, I have never known her spend half an hour in listless idleness, or indulge herself in any book or amusement when there was any thing else that should be done. Here she comes now, with her work-basket full of stockings to be looked over, though I know she would like much better to go on with Irving's Life of Washington."

"Mrs. Oldham, my dear," continued the Doctor, addressing his wife, as she came into the room, "I have just been obeying the Holy Scriptures in regard to you."

"How is that, husband?" said Mrs. Oldham, in reply.

"I have been praising you, my dear."

"Is that a Scriptural duty?"

"To be sure it is. Don't you remember the place where the Bible speaks of the virtuous woman and of her husband praising her?"

"But what is such a woman to do, if she have no husband to praise her?" said Mrs. Oldham.

"But the passage supposes she has," said the Doctor in reply. "Besides," he added, "the very meaning of the word in the original tongue is wife and housemother."

"But," replied Mrs. Oldham, it is only said 'her husband—he praiseth her;' does that necessarily imply that her husband is bound to praise her?"

"Certainly, my dear, if you look to the whole of it. It says also that 'she SHALL BE PRAISED;' and says it in a way which means that praise is her due, and surely due from her husband—one would say so even if he were not expressly named as the person that was to praise her."

"But does it mean that *my* husband is to praise *me?*" said Mrs. Oldham.

"To be sure it does; for you are a virtuous woman, a good wife and housemother. The housewifely virtues of the nineteenth century differ in their form from those of the days of Solomon; but the essence of them is the same. And you, my dear, possess, in the form befitting an American wife of the present day, all the virtues of King Lemuel's mother's pattern woman—except that you do not keep your lamp burning all night and get up before day—a virtue I would not like you to possess. You are not an early riser, but when you are up, I am sure Lemuel's mother could not wish for a more exemplary model of industry, of cheerful household energy and cleverness—after the fashion of modern times. You do not indeed 'lay hands to the spindle,' nor your 'hands hold the distaff'—those once indispensable and commendable implements of feminine industry being now obsolete ; but your exploits with the scissors and needle are a fair and proper offset. Nor can it be said of you, as of Lemuel's mother's heroine—

. . . . . 'She maketh fine linen and selleth it.'

"But then you *make up* the linen which you buy, and that is a great deal more than most women nowadays do—and a saving of expense to me, perhaps a sufficient saving ; for the domestic manufacture of linen is gone out of vogue because the mills, I believe, make it the cheapest. Neither are you one who

. . . . . 'delivereth girdles unto the merchant,'

home-made girdles (whatever they were) in barter for furbelows you cannot make ; but then you are mostly content with such furbelows as you can make—which comes pretty nearly to the same thing. And as to the rest, hearken to 'the words of King Lemuel, and the Prophecy that his mother taught him' concerning the virtuous wife :

> 'For her price is far above rubies :
> The heart of her husband doth safely trust in her,
> So that he shall have no need of spoil'—

"No need, that is, of making forays upon the flocks of neighboring tribes, or of plundering travelling caravans—the Oriental mode of stocking the larder and replenishing the purse, equivalent to the modern practice of burglary, or going upon the road, or at least (which is about the same in morals) of seeking the 'spoils of office' to make the pot boil—a necessity from which I count it a blessed thing the thrift of my wife exempts me.

"But hearken further :

> 'She will do him good and not evil
> All the days of her life.
> . . . .
> She stretcheth out her hand to the poor,
> Yea, she reacheth forth her hands to the needy.
> She is not afraid of snow for her household ;
> For all her household are clothed with double garments.
> . . . .

> She openeth her mouth with wisdom:
> And in her tongue is the law of kindness.
> She looketh well to the ways of her household,
> And eateth not the bread of idleness.
> Her children rise up and call her blessed;
> Her husband also; and he praiseth her, saying,
> ' *Many daughters have done virtuously,*
> *But thou excellest them all!*
> *Favor is deceitful, and beauty is vain;*
> *But a woman that feareth the* LORD—SHE SHALL BE PRAISED.
> *Give her the fruit of her hands;*
> *And let her own works praise her in the gates.*'

"There, Mrs. Oldham, that is you. And now go to your work-basket and stockings, and let Lilly learn to be like her mother."

"Oh, what nonsense you talk, husband," said Mrs. Oldham, laughing. "My work-basket and stockings! Elevated objects for which to live! A noble usefulness, indeed!"

"Rail not, my dear," said the Doctor,—"rail not even jestingly at the homeliness of your duties. The smallest, homeliest, humblest actions are ennobled by the sentiment of love and duty. Think of the two archangels—one sent to rule the British realm, the other to sweep the streets of London, and both finding equal dignity and equal pleasure in the faithful doing of their work. Bethink you too with what joyous alacrity the cherubim would grind knives along the streets of our town, if set to do it by their Lord and ours; and how well they would grind them too! And not a single seraph, winging by on swift pinions upon some embassy of highest import to the realm-ruling angel, would have a thought of scorn for the faithful knife-grinder's, or the cheerful street-sweeper's place and work.

"Look then upon your work-basket as a badge of dignity, and upon your scissors and needles as holy implements. Shirt-making is sacred. Stocking-mending is divine.

"But I know your heart, my dear wife. Would you neglect your work-basket in order to be directress or secretary to the Society for planting a Christian coffee-growing colony at Borioboola Gha on the left bank of the Niger? No, you would not, my dear.

"Would you let my shirts and Phil's go without buttons, in order that you might make flannel shirts for the benighted dwellers in Timbuctoo? No, my dear wife, you would not.

"Would you let your children go about without warm stockings to their feet, in order that you might go about begging money to buy warming-pans for the children of the tropics, or even to buy

Mount Vernon at ten times its proper price? No, Mrs. Oldham, my dearest wife, I know you better. When your work-basket is cleared, you will go and carry comfort and coals to poor sickly Mrs. Johnson, who has three children to maintain, and no way to do it but making pantaloons for the slop-shops at eighteen cents the pair. And you will find more honor and more pleasure in it than in uniting all the offices of the Ladies' Mount Vernon Association in your own single person.

"And Lilly, my dear child, I hope you will always be of your mother's way of thinking."

"But surely, husband, you don't object to the Mount Vernon Association, and ladies holding office in it?"

"No, my dear, not at all. The object is noble. I am only mortified and ashamed for my country that this should be the way of accomplishing it— that it should be left to the women to gather together in such ways the money that ought to have been appropriated long ago by the nation. One million (out of the twenty that have been probably wasted this very year, in jobs corruptly given to President-making politicians) would have been an ample provision for the purpose.

"No, my dear, it may be as fitting, as it is necessary, for some women to hold office in this association : only it is not your vocation, any more than it would be mine to go about lecturing in its behalf —even if I could draw together such audiences as Everett delights."

CHAPTER XV.

WHEREIN THE DOCTOR SAYS PSHAW TO SOMETHING ADVANCED BY THE AUTHOR, AND ADVANCES HIS OWN NOTIONS.—COMFORT AND SWILL NOT THE HIGHEST FELICITY FOR RATIONAL BEINGS.—THE WORLD NEEDS MARTYRS, BUT CROOKE RACKET NOT THE RIGHT TYPE.

The Doctor is not of a turn of mind that disposes him to think as other people think, and to do as they do merely because they think so and do so. He accepts nothing—save coin, bank-notes, whatever passes for money—because it has the stamp of conventional acceptance, nor at the common valuation, unless it coincides with his own estimate of its intrinsic worth. Popular suffrages do not seem to have with him the weight they have with most persons, and are perhaps entitled to, particularly in regard to the public personages of the age; indeed, I am afraid—if the truth must be confessed—that the admiring acclamation of all Boston would not of itself be enough to convince him that this man was a great man, statesman, and patriot, that one a great true poet, or the other one a great genuine thinker and inspired prophet—the rather as he has, besides, noted that great men, bards, and prophets have in their generation been sometimes undiscovered, sometimes vilified, and sometimes even crucified, while charlatans and impostors have carried off the praises and prizes of the age. In short, it matters not greatly to him what the general opinion is, so far as the forming of his own is concerned. If he thinks as other people do, it is not so much because they think so, as because he has come to think so on grounds of his own.

In all this the Doctor is simply and unconsciously honest. There is nothing of self-conceit, caprice, love of paradox, vanity, or pride of independence in him. He is no more inclined to reject than to accept the prevailing opinion merely because it is the prevailing opinion; and whether he agrees with the world or differs from it—in either case it is simply because he cannot help it. As to the rest, there is nothing of arrogance, bitterness, or intolerance in his nature.

Professor Clare, unlike the Doctor, is always in happy sympathy with the prevailing opinion.

Whatever all the world—his world, the "highest respectability" world—thinks, he thinks. Its creed is his creed, its law his law—not through reflection or any process of thought, but spontaneously, in an altogether unconscious way. It is just the constitution of his mind that he should, in all simplicity and godly sincerity, be of the same way of thinking with the world around him.

It may not argue a high order of mind, or a very great force of character, but I confess I am apt to look upon this disposition of honest sympathy with the spirit of one's age, as on several accounts a felicity and a good fortune: it is such a saving of labor and trouble, and procures so many advantages of popular favor and good-will. I say honest sympathy—and I lay stress upon it; for as there is nothing more despicable than hypocritical compliances prompted by a mere sharp look-out or mean instinct of selfishness, so I should be sorry to be thought capable of regarding any advantages thus acquired as a genuine felicity and a true good fortune.

But as for that thoroughly honest sympathy which goes spontaneously along with the popular current, in perfect good faith without any selfish ends—there is certainly nothing dishonorable in it, and so the advantages that follow it are not against equity and right. What if the world does bestow equal favor upon the make-believe allegiance of the mean and base? That argues, indeed, a want of discrimination in the world—also a universe somewhat out of joint; but is it any reason why Professor Clare should not enjoy advantages which in his case are not the rewards of baseness and meanness? And these advantages are so many and various that—as I said—I am prone to think it a good fortune whenever they can be honestly enjoyed. We all know what a favorite he generally is who is unaffectedly pleased with everybody; and when one sees with the world's eyes, holds with the world's faith, and walks in the world's ways, he is in the way of receiving a thousand tokens of the world's good-will. Besides, it is so much more pleasant to go with the stream. Independently of the favor one meets with, one gets over the ground with more ease and speed if his path lies in the same direction all the world is moving in, and has also the sense of companionship, which is comfortable when one likes his company.

"Pshaw," said the Doctor, to whom I was making these remarks about the Professor the other day—"you are trying your hand at 'considering too curiously;' but the game is not worth the candle, it is analysis wasted, whether you really think as you say, or only amuse yourself with saying so. It is well enough for Professor Clare to be what he honestly is—seeing he cannot be any thing else—and to enjoy the consequences of being so, if they are matters of enjoyment to him. But let the dead bury their dead. How would it go with a world filled only with Professor Clares? It would fare ill for human progress. Where would be the discoverers and inventors, the heroes and reformers?"

"Well," said I, "I was not setting up the Professor as the highest type of a man—I should be loath to stand godfather to his achieving any heroic exploits. But you must admit there are many inconveniences, discomforts, and perils in being too much ahead of one's age, or in standing out all alone against it. Think of it. Even in our own times, through what obstacles had George Stephenson to fight his way: visionary madman, fool, quack, charlatan, impostor, were the mildest judgments he encountered from the highest scientific and practical authorities retained against him by the wealth and social influence of his country. How the pompous wise ones of Fulton's day shook their empty heads in solemn derision of his visionary ideas. Think of Columbus struggling for eighteen years, amidst poverty, obloquy, contempt, and insult, against the learning, science and religion of his times, for leave to give a new world to the old one."

"What of that?" said the Doctor; "they were better off than the Clares of their times."

"You mean they conquered success, triumph, and the world's recognition at last," I rejoined.

"No: independently of that," replied the Doctor, "they were better off in the midst of their trials. Exemption from discomforts and the enjoyment of the world's sweet voices is not the highest style of happiness."

"Well, I suppose, then, it is not worth while," I continued, "to remind you of poor old Galileo in the dungeons of the inquisition for being so much wiser than the wisdom of his age,—nor of Socrates in prison compelled to drink hemlock for the same reason."

"What of that?" returned the Doctor; "dungeons and hemlock are by no means the worst things that can befall a man, unless it be a truth that man was made only for comfort and swill. Only as to poor old Galileo, he was not quite as brave as Socrates; if he had been, he might have been a martyr of equal reverence—such as the world has frequent need of."

"Need of martyrs?" said I.

"Yes, sir," replied the Doctor, "the world cannot get on without them—cannot otherwise well be brought to a stand on any perilously downhill course. No sacred cause especially can thrive well without martyrs."

"But you would not have a man go about battling the world, and inviting martyrdom, like Crooke Racket?" said I.

"No," replied the Doctor, "a reformer ought to be wise as well as brave. If a man has a great sacred cause to carry against the world, a wise discretion will often prompt many compliances and seeming compliances—reserves and withholdings—in order to get the world at advantage. But Crooke Racket does not know the wisdom of reserves and 'brilliant flashes of silence'—as Sidney Smith says—judiciously interposed between the gleams of his artillery. If he knew how to prepare a good mortar bed, and get a good raking position, he might make a wonderful crashing among the shams and falsities of the age. But he fires off a forty-eight pounder right into a whirlwind, when he ought to know it could not have the slightest effect to stop it. He runs his head plump against a stone wall, when he ought to expect nothing for it but a broken skull. He calls the world mad, in a way and under circumstances that, if he had an ounce of discretion, he would see could not possibly result in any thing else than the world returning the compliment by a vote so overwhelming as to leave him in a minority of one: and then because the world does outvote him, he likens himself to Luther, St. Paul, and even to Him of whom the Jews and His own kindred said He had a Devil, and was beside Himself. But Crooke Racket is a fool; and a reformer has no business to be a fool: only there is no law of the land against it—none but the law of the moral universe, that if a man will be a fool, he must take the consequences."

"How many men of great parts does egotism spoil for true reformers and good martyrs."

CHAPTER XVI.

LOT'S HOUSE IN SODOM.—JONAH IN NEW YORK.—THE DOCTOR VILIFIES UNIVERSAL SUFFRAGE AND AN ELECTIVE JUDICIARY IN A VERY SHOCKING WAY; AND MAKES THE MOST UNSUPPOSABLE SUPPOSITIONS.—AN EXTRAORDINARY TICKET FOR CITY OFFICERS.

"MY DEAR," said the Doctor one evening, looking across the table to his wife, who was at the moment absorbed in a volume of Macaulay's History, "can you tell me the street and number of Lot's house in *Sodom?*"

"Bless me, husband, what makes you ask that question?" said Mrs. Oldham.

"Why, my dear, I have just been writing the address on my letter to your brother John, and I perceive I have directed it to West Twenty-First street, *Sodom*, and that made me think of Lot, and how near neighbors he and your brother might be."

"I think, mother," said Phil, whose attention was drawn by this talk from the page of Chitty he was poring over, "you ought solemnly to remind my father that Lot is dead, and therefore he and Uncle John can't possibly be neighbors."

Phil was an incipient lawyer and a presumptive judge—but at present much given to setting small witticisms on the back of other people's remarks.

"Phil is like the celebrated Fox," said the Doctor. . . .

"I am glad it's not the celebrated Goose," said Phil in an undertone. "I confess to being unsound on that."

. . . . "Or the celebrated somebody else," continued the Doctor, not heeding the interruption, "of whom the great Pitt or the witty Sheridan—I shall not decide which—said he drew on his imagination for his facts and on his memory for his wit. Phil's draft on his memory in this case, however, is a good one. Charles Lamb's four Scotchmen, springing up at once to set him right as to the unreasonableness of wishing for Burns's presence at the dinner-table, instead of his son's, is one of Lamb's characteristic and exquisite touches of humor. If his Scotchmen were here, Phil, they would perhaps have reminded me not only that Lot is dead, but also that he moved out of Sodom some time before his death, and before your Uncle John moved in."

"But let me look at your letter, husband," said Mrs. Oldham.

He handed it to her.

"I see," said she, "you have got it down in your largest letters. It all comes from your always calling New York Sodom. Are you not ashamed to give such an ill name to my native place?"

"Father's bump of veneration is not large," said Phil; "you ought not, mother, to be hurt at any thing he says. He has been heard to speak very disrespectfully of his own native place; and I shouldn't be surprised to hear him call the capital of his country Tophet."

"Humph,—draft on Sidney Smith this time," said the Doctor. "But touching your native town, Mrs. Oldham, you have done it a great deal too much honor by being born there—though it was not then the Sodom it is now. It is a great consolation to me that you are so much better than your native place. It is not worthy of you; and it has no proper appreciation of your worth. You are naturally unable to think ill of any body or any thing, and like all such good and kind-hearted persons as you are, you have, no doubt, many tender memories of the scenes of your early years: and so, I sometimes think you are not quite thankful enough for the privilege of being out of that bad place."

"I am sure, husband, I don't wish to go back there to live," said Mrs. Oldham.

"I am heartily glad of it, my dear," replied the Doctor. "I should be inconsolably afflicted, if it were otherwise. If indeed it were possible—I know it is not, and I put it merely as a monstrous supposition—that you could desert your husband and go down there to live, after being once fairly out of the place, I should be filled with the most distressing apprehensions. It would imply in fact an awful change in your nature, and would justify the worst forebodings. Why, Lot's wife would be a model woman compared with you. She never once set foot in Sodom after she left it with Lot. *Could not stir to go back*—do you say? There is no proof she wanted to go back, or would have done so if she had not been stiffened into a pillar of salt. *Looked back*—did she? Well, what of that? That don't begin to prove that she wanted to go back, or would have tried to go if she had not been so fast fixed. It only proves that she wanted to get a glimpse of Sodom, merely to see how things were going on there. Pardonable curiosity in a woman, particularly if you consider the smoke and sulphurous smell. Pardonable, I say it seems to me. But she was punished even for that—stiffened into a pillar of salt, and planted there forever. And if she was thus dealt with for merely looking back, what and how much more dreadful must have been her fate, if she had wanted to go back, or had tried to go back, or had actually deserted her husband and gone back! Think of it, my dear wife! It makes me shudder."

"There, that will do, husband: you have talked all this nonsense because I want to spend the Christmas holidays with my mother. Surely you do not wish me not to go?"

"No my dear—you have a mother living in Sodom. It does not appear that Lot's wife had. I cannot object to a short visit of filial piety. I shall calmly await your return. I cannot but believe the city will be spared till you are safely out."

"Well, take your letter then, and put it into a new envelope. Costs you that, and another stamp. Serves you right for talking such absurd stuff."

"No, Mrs. Oldham, I am not going to lose my envelope, or my stamp. Remember who it was that said 'a penny saved is twopence earned,' and 'a pin a day's a groat a year'—which latter frugal truth comes specially home to the business and bosoms of your sex, my dear, who mostly use that abominable substitute for honest fastenings. I do not know whether that profane wag who divided the human race into men, women, and clergymen, has laid down the differential or distinguishing peculiarity of each several sort, but I am sure the definition of woman should be a pin-using animal. No, my dear, I shall waste no envelope, no stamp. I shall just run my pen through the word Sodom, and put New York under it, thus:

J. S. Borton, M.D.

750 W. 21st St.

~~Sodom~~
New York.

"Who knows what wholesome thoughts and fears leading to repentance and postponement of impending fate, its perusal by corrupt officials—clerks and carriers, may lead to. It may be like Jonah's preaching that saved Nineveh. It is not to be supposed that the sound of the prophet's voice reached the ears of all the Ninevites. His warnings were repeated by those who heard them, and so spread out all over the city. A little leaven leaveneth the whole lump. It would almost make me hopeful for the salvation of your native place, wicked as it is, but that I remember democratic institutions did not prevail in Nineveh; and so when the Lord bid them repent, and the King bid them betake themselves to sackcloth and prayers, following his example, the people did as they were bid, and were saved. But catch the democracy of New Sodom tolerating any such interference with their sovereign power. Do you think Jonah would be safe there? Wall Street might be too busy, Fifth Avenue too fine, to heed him or to harm him. But could he traverse the Sixth Ward unhurt? Would he not wish himself safe in the whale's belly before he got clear of Corlear's Hook? The 'Bowery Boys' would they not convert him into a bag of sore bones? And ten to one, would not some 'Dead Rabbit' leader *finish* him with six inches of inevitable dirk knife?

"And in such a case what do you think would become of the murderer? Hanged—do you say? Not a bit of it. He is far too useful in other ways to be put to such a use as that. Let that be for friendless negroes, and those who have no political influence. But this fellow is a citizen, a free voter, and at the head of a large band of powerful and well-armed voters—can control the result at half a dozen polls, through his skill and prowess in bringing up the right and keeping away the wrong sort of votes. He has no fears. He knows who have the making of all the public authorities, except the police, and mean to have the making of them again soon—for 'tis insufferable usurpation to deprive them of their indefeasable right of having every thing their own way. The police may arrest him That is all they can do. He must be committed indeed, and go through the forms of law. It is the wisest course. It is attended with no danger, and it secures to rogues of the right sort other advantages besides deliverance from the penalties of crime. It is good policy also in a larger view. It keeps up a show of justice and public order, and makes a great many pawns on the political chessboard more contentedly passive in the hands of the players, and so strengthens our incomparable free institutions. The ingenuities of the process furnish, moreover, a highly pleasurable variety of excitement to his friends and followers—to all sporting men, fancy boys, the keepers and frequenters of those drinking and gambling places that are so fitly termed hells.

"By all means then let the murderer be delivered in due course of law. A purse shall be made up, and the smartest lawyers retained. Justice Sharpclaw shall send the man to prison. He understands his part. Judge Wrestright shall grant a writ of *habeas corpus*. He cannot let the prisoner off with *a fine of one dollar;* for he has not been contented this time with beating his victim half dead; nor can he admit him to bail in the sum of five hundred dollars, although Alderman Poteen, keeper of the gambling house in the Flash ward, and Alderman O'Floggerty, emigrant runner, both famous for election fights, knocking down policemen, and the like exploits, are urgent to go his sureties. But if thought best, a sharp skirmish of writs and counter-writs shall take place, and during the intervals of proceedings the police in charge of him shall, on the intimation of the Judge, and for a due consideration, obligingly accompany him to his favorite haunts, and permit him to solace himself with champagne, brandy-smashers, and the smiles of the fair and frail. When the day of trial comes, if the judges should forget on whom they depend for re-election, the jury shall be found a safe reliance—that shall be well cared for. They will never agree in a verdict of guilty; and so poor Jonah's murderer shall come safely off—the object of higher admiration ever after to his band, as the boy that *settled* that prating old prophet who was disturbing the city!"

"O husband, how you run on," said Mrs. Oldham. "You take as much delight in wilful hyperbole as your *quondam* friend Sidney Smith. But I know what abatement to make."

"Make none in this case, my dear," replied the Doctor. "This is not the rollicking humor of exaggeration. My fiction falls short of facts. The records of the last three years more than bear me out. No, Mrs. Oldham, there is no salvation for your native town while universal suffrage and an elective judiciary prevail there."

"I am glad Professor Clare is not here to hear you say that," said Mrs. Oldham.

"Professor Clare, my dear, has a great deal more softness of heart than clearness of head, and however shocked he might be at my opinions, you wouldn't need feel any alarm for my safety, if he were here—which is more than I can assure you of, if I were to go down and proclaim my thoughts freely about the streets, in the primary meetings, and at the polls of your native town. Be comforted, however: I shall not do so. I shall take warning from Jonah's fate."

"But, husband, Professor Clare says it is all along of your English prejudices, the way you disparage free institutions."

"Professor Clare, my good little wife, is our neighbor, a worthy and kind-hearted man, for whom I entertain a very friendly regard, which nothing that he is ever likely to do or say will diminish. But Professor Clare is Professor Clare. He is an excellent Greek scholar, but he is not an historical philosopher, nor a philosophical statesman; nor is he, so far as I have observed, a person who does his own thinking. His opinions on the most important subjects were adopted, not formed, and are of the sort most current in the circle of those with whom he lived at the time when men like him lay in their stock of opinions. Consequently he is a firm believer in democratic institutions, in the divine right of a free and enlightened people to recognize no higher law than their own will, and in the glorious future of our great republic, its 'manifest destiny' to overrun and annex every thing that borders on it.

"But Professor Clare is mistaken in regard to my English prejudices, as you could have informed him."

"I did so," said Mrs. Oldham. "I told him that notwithstanding your English education, your prepossessions and prejudices were all in favor of our institutions when you came back; and I told him, too," she added, with a gentle kindling of her placid eye, and a little flush slightly heightening the early-autumn peach bloom on her cheek, "that however sorry you were to see any thing going on in a wrong way, your love for your native country is as true and as warm as ever beat in any man's breast—and it was that very love which made you so quick to feel whatever might bring disgrace or danger to us."

"Bravo! little woman," said the Doctor, with a smile.

'Lives there a man with soul so dead,'

"or woman either, the poet might have said, only it was needless—all women becoming men in certain poetical cases, just as they all become 'dearly

8

beloved brethren,' in the Prayer Book ; although I confess I always felt a little awkward in addressing them so, when they were the only brethren at church—not an uncommon case at Wednesday and Friday prayers. But where am I wandering ? Oh, I was going to say you are right, my little, best friend ; I am wedded to my country as I am to you, 'for better for worse,' and my heart is faithful to my vows ; although it is proper for me to add that I have found it all better and no worse, as regards you, Mrs. Oldham.

"I do not disparage free institutions—by which Professor Clare means our own institutions, for he has no notion that there are any other free ones than ours ;—I only fear there is not virtue enough among us to make universal suffrage and an elective judiciary safe. I am sure they will·not do for our great cities."

"Well, husband, I am very sorry you cannot be more hopeful for my native city."

"So am I. I like to hope for what I greatly wish for," said the Doctor, "and still more for what you wish for ; but my eyes and my reason will not always let me do as I like."

"But there are a great many good and excellent persons there—that is one comfort."

"True, my dear, you and I know a great many, and there are a great many more that we don't know—enough, as you see, to save it thus far: and unless they move out of it, as you and I have done, it may stand for some time yet. But it may be a real Sodom, for all that; growing wickeder every day, and as sure to be destroyed, sooner or later, as Old Sodom was—although not in the same fashion perhaps; for the Almighty does not seem, since then, to have taken that method of destroying wicked cities—unless the fate of those two Roman towns that were overwhelmed by the burning lava of Vesuvius be set down as examples of the same sort. They are mostly left to work out their own destruction, after a certain Kilkenny-cat fashion; except when some strong-handed fellow comes in and puts a stop to the process by grape-shot, like him of the *Eighteenth of Brumaire* in Paris—which sort of salvation cannot so well be hoped for in the case of New Sodom, owing to the peculiar constitution of the State and General Government of the country.

"Doubtless, as you say, there are a great many good people there. But how much good does their goodness do? Does it control the city government? Does it turn the scale at elections? Does it put good men into office? Does it stop the progress of corruption?

"What does it do even to reclaim and convert the vicious and dangerous classes?

"It goes to church itself—it fills up a great many comfortable, a great many magnificent churches every Sunday. But how many places of Christian worship, of the humblest sort, does it provide for the poor and sinful in the quarters where the rulers of the city mostly live? It gives ample incomes—a fine house, and five, six, or seven thousand dollars a year—to its own favorite preachers; but how many preachers does it maintain whom one thousand dollars a year would enable with gladness to carry the Gospel, and their own warm hearts with it, down into the damp cellars, and up under sharp-roofed garrets, to thousands who otherwise would never hear its voice?

"I speak not merely of the Pharisees—the highest class of professors of godliness—the long-garmented and broad-phylacteried, who, with their wives and children, fill up the sumptuous churches in the fashionable streets and squares, and thank God they are not like the publicans and sinners—which is all they care for them. It is not of such that I speak. There are a great many truly good, loving and gentle-hearted persons, who are really sorry there should be any wickedness or unhappiness in the world, and desirous to do all they can to make everybody as well off and as good as themselves—who yet make a very mistaken use of their goodness; partly because they are more afraid than our Lord was of coming into contact with poor sinners—which they need not be if their love was as great as his,—and partly because they have been wrongly guided, and so are very earnest in works of love for the Feejee Island heathen, and overlook the Manhattan Island heathen in the midst of them —are very liberal of their money to build churches in the new western States, and to send missionaries to China, while they forget that there are large districts of their own city—the abodes of filth and vice—where churches and missionaries are at least as much needed, and which it should, at all events, be their first care to supply."

"But, husband, there are a great many persons of wealth and influence there now fully awake to this need."

"Let them go earnestly to work, then," said the Doctor, "if they would save the city. It is in a bad way now, and universal suffrage and a judiciary elected at short intervals only make things worse.

Why, suppose the Good Lord were to nominate Gabriel for Mayor, and a choice list of other good angels for Aldermen, Common Councilmen, and Judges, and promise the people a good city government without a penny's cost; do you think the ticket would be elected?"

"Dear me, husband, what a case to put! But can you doubt it would be?"

"I hope it would, my dear, but depend upon it there would be an opposition ticket."

"Ha! ha!" cried Phil, "imagine the placards headed, 'PURE DEMOCRATIC TICKET;' and the inscriptions on the street banners: '*No Theocracy;*' '*No Church and State;*' '*A Human Government for Human Beings;*' and the speeches made in the Ward meetings on these watchwords and the foul language heaped upon Gabriel and the other good angels in the drinking-shops."

"Stop, Phil," said Mrs. Oldham, "that is shocking; you are worse than your father."

"I think we've had enough," said the Doctor. "Only this I will say, that unless the goodness that is in the city can get control of the city government and put good men into office, it will no more avail to its salvation, than Lot's righteousness did to Old Sodom's. The good people will be got out of it in some way—led out by their good angels, like our agreeable neighbors, the Pelhams, who have just come up here to our great delight, or driven out by the violence of the wicked, and the city will inevitably go down to chaos, destruction, and the devil."

CHAPTER XVII.

A SHORT CHAPTER ON JUDGE-MAKING—NOT AMUSING; AND NOT SO LIKELY TO BE INTERESTING TO THOSE WHO NEED, AS TO THOSE WHO DO NOT NEED, THE INSTRUCTION IT CONTAINS.

"You are in favor, then, of our present way of making judges by universal-suffrage ballot-box elections?" asked the Doctor.

The subject came up between him and Professor Clare, a few days after the talk recorded in the last chapter.

The Professor said he was.

"You go also for a limited term of office—for frequent elections at short intervals, instead of the old tenure?"

The Professor approved of that too. It was—he thought—in accordance with the genius of our institutions. That is a phrase he is greatly pleased with, and one he often uses. If any thing falls—or seems to him to fall—within its application, that of itself is enough to commend it to his judgment and approval.

"Genius of our institutions!" replied the Doctor; "will that make a foolish thing a wise one, or console us for its working badly? Don't you see it is against all human nature that such a tenure of judicial office should work well?"

The Professor confessed he did not see it.

"Well," continued the Doctor, "there was a time in England when all the judges were not only appointed by the crown, but held their office at the mere good pleasure of the king, who could at any moment remove them by his absolute will. But in the time of WILLIAM the THIRD it became an established part of the British Constitution, that they should hold office during good behavior— though in practice their commissions were considered as vacated upon a demise of the crown as late as the reign of George the Third, when, at the earnest recommendation of that sovereign, this cause of vacancy was done away with, and the tenure of judicial office was made perfect during good behavior, with an ample and dignified official salary absolutely secured. You think this an improvement on the old way, don't you?"

"O yes, it was a great triumph for British liberties, a noble security for the rights of the people."

"How so?"

"Because it made the judges independent of the crown," replied the Professor.

"But wherein lies the worth and importance of that independence?" asked the Doctor.

"Why," said the Professor, "it freed the judges from temptations to pervert the course of justice, in order to suit the royal pleasure, and afforded the best guaranties for the upright and impartial administration of the laws."

"True," replied the Doctor, "and yet you don't see that the same principles in human nature require that the judges should be equally independent of the popular as of the royal will?"

The Professor looked puzzled, as if taken a little aback.

"Are judges," added the Doctor, "any more likely to be upright and impartial when they depend for continuance in office upon the will of the people, than when they depend upon the good pleasure of a king?"

The Professor's face cleared up. He was sure—he said—they were.

"Well," replied the Doctor, "that is a mere

question of comparison and degree not worth deciding: for even if it be as you say—though I don't believe it—would that at all impair the truth of the general principle which makes the independence of the judiciary of the highest importance to the impartial administration of the laws? The true question is: whether it is not best for the purity and integrity of the judges that they should be freed from all dependence upon the mere arbitrary pleasure of any body, whether of a single or a multitudinous sovereign, and so freed from all temptations and respects of fear or favor?"

The Professor made no reply.

"My dear sir," continued the Doctor, "don't talk any more about the genius of our institutions, as if that was necessarily conclusive of any thing. What is the use of being duped by phrases? There is a great deal of human nature in man. What matters a fine theory if it is not adapted to human nature under its actual conditions?

"Besides, the way of making judges you approve of is not—rightly considered—fine in theory: it violates a great principle lying at the bottom of the matter—a principle the bulk of the people have no perception of, and which you and thousands of others like you, who ought to be more clear-headed, do not seem to see."

"What is that?"

"Why, that the sovereign should never sit on the bench itself. It is essentially tyrannical, incompatible with any proper security for righteous judgment. I suppose you see that it must be so in an absolute monarchy, where the sovereign power is vested in a single person?"

"Yes," the Professor said, "that is very clear."

"It has always been so held," said the Doctor, "by the wise in all modern times, even under the most absolute governments of Europe; and neither Louis the Fourteenth, nor Frederick the Great, ever dared face their people with a denial of the principle, however they may in any case have overborne it in practice.

"Yet you are in favor of a way of making judges which virtually puts not even the sovereign—bad in principle as that is—but a majority on the bench. But there is always tyranny, always danger to justice, where the holder of the supreme power—be it Louis the Fourteenth or the majority—either sits in judgment or controls or influences it in the courts.

"I do not approve of the judges being elected by the people: but I do not think the mode of their appointment matters so much, provided they hold during good behavior. But to make their continuance in office dependent at short intervals upon a popular vote, is bad in principle, and so it cannot but work badly—especially in our great cities, like the one down below.

"Think of it : judges elected every little while —on the same ticket perhaps with political officers —at any rate the nominations always controlled by party managers—the balance of power in the hands of that sort of human nature which is always to be found in such large proportions in great cities, and which is always likely to be most prominent and powerful in politics and elections, at primary meetings and at the polls ;—gracious heavens ! What must not the administration of justice in time come to ? What has it not come to now ? Where is that certainty of punishment following crime which the wisdom of criminal jurisprudence and the good of society demands ? There is almost nothing of it left. It is scarcely possible to bring a criminal who has money or political influence within the compass of the penalties of the law.

"I do not say that all the evils in the working of our judicial system come merely from the bad tenure of office of the judges. Some of them come from, and all of them are aggravated by, the unwise multiplication of judges and courts. Hence you see court interfering with court, and judge with judge—a perfect war of writs and counter-writs; and what with the practical working of the law on jury-forming and on admissible evidence, the administration of justice is well-nigh reduced to a game of legal thimble-rigging between sharp lawyers. It is almost a bounty on crime, a proclamation of immunity to the criminal.

"No, sir, our way of making judges does not work well; it will go on to work worse and worse; and justice will never have free course until the people become wise enough to put good and fit men upon the bench without regard to party politics, and to make them independent of the popular favor for their continuance there.

"Of which there is small hope."

CHAPTER XVIII.

SOMETHING ON UNIVERSAL SUFFRAGE AND SACRED RIGHTS—WHEREIN IS SEEN HOW PROFESSOR CLARE AND PELHAM BRIEF DIFFER FROM EACH OTHER, AND THE DOCTOR FROM THEM BOTH.

"How many persons among us," said the Doctor, after a pause, "talk as if all rights were sacred—almost the only sacred things in the universe, and political rights the most sacred, and the exercise of them the chief end of man.

"There's my friend Pelham Brief—I tried the other day to make him comprehend the difference between a right resting merely in prescription, and a right grounded in natural justice."

"Yet Brief is a man of genius," said Professor Clare.

"Yes," replied the Doctor, "Brief is a man of genius—in his way. He has a truly creative imagination; and he has withal a fancy so rich and bright, a taste so pure and delicate, and so exquisite a faculty of expression, that I reckon him one of our most charming writers. But there are a good many sorts of genius. Plato was a man of genius. Brief has not the same sort of genius Plato had, any more than he probably has the genius of Cæsar, or Richelieu, or George Stephenson. He is a man of genius in the poetic sphere, in the world of fine letters; but not in the world of thought. He has no eminent faculty for science, analysis, logical connection, theoretic insight, or higher speculation. He doesn't seize at a glance the principles that underlie and connect political doctrines, and determine the truth or falsehood of theories on human rights. He cannot see but the right of suffrage—because it is called a right—must of necessity be a sacred right, belonging therefore to every human being, as much as the right of life and liberty, and consequently to deprive any person of it, unless it be forfeited by crime, is a moral wrong, or, as the political orators say, an atrocious violation of the sacred principles of eternal justice."

"But I agree with Brief," said Professor Clare. "I go for universal suffrage."

"What do you mean by universal?"

"Why, all the people voting, of course."

"Negroes?"

"Hem—no, I did not mean them."

"Women?"

"No—I don't go for that."

"Ah, by universal then you mean all the white men! A droll idea of universal! And a still droller idea of a sacred right—one which the largest number of full-grown persons in the State may be—and probably are—excluded from! But why should not negroes and women vote?"

"Oh, it would not do," the Professor said.

"But they are human persons," insisted the Doctor, "and as virtuous and intelligent, and as capable of voting uprightly and wisely, as the great mass of the voters in general, and of our Irish and German citizens in particular."

"But it would not work well," replied the Professor.

"But who is to decide that question?" said the Doctor.

"The majority of the people, of course," was the Professor's answer.

"The majority of male white people, you mean?"

"Yes."

"But don't you see," said the Doctor, "if you allow the majority may justly make one restriction to-day, they may make another to-morrow—may exclude, for instance, all but native-born citizens, or all who are not freeholders, or all such gray-haired old fellows as I am;—in short, don't you see your boasted right of universal suffrage resolves itself at last into the right of a majority—it may be a majority of one—to deprive everybody else of a right you set out with assuming to be sacred, and claiming should on that account be universal?

"Besides: consider how droll it is to call that a sacred right which you yet make depend for its rightful existence on the opinion of a majority as to the expediency of allowing it. Is that the tenure by which you and I hold our right to live and to dispose of ourselves? Should we not say to any majority that proposed to grant us the right to life and to self-ownership: Thank you for nothing;— our right to these things is anterior to your grant and independent of it—something you can indeed recognize, something you are bound to protect, and which, within the limits of justice and for good ends, you may regulate the exercise of, but which you cannot give, nor (unless forfeited by crime) take away, except by unjust force? Does it not seem to you to be thus in respect to life and liberty?"

The Professor said surely it did seem to him to be so, and impossible it should be otherwise.

"You cannot, then," continued the Doctor, "conceive that any notion of convenience or advantage to the State, nor even any persuasion of State necessity—however honest and strong—would make it right for the majority to put you and me to death, or shut us up in prison, without any fault or crime on our part?"

"No, certainly, I cannot."

"Well, if it holds thus in regard to life and liberty, must it not hold thus in regard to the right of suffrage also, if it be equally a sacred right? Must it not be equally independent of the grant of a majority? Must it not be a right that no innocent person, capable of exercising it, can be rightfully deprived of at the mere will of any majority, however large? Must it not be one which, though it may be forced to succumb to the immoral law of the strongest, yet will—even while the foot of violence is crushing it—proclaim itself inviolable?"

"My dear sir," continued the Doctor, "it will not do for you to talk of universal suffrage, when you mean only male whites,—nor to talk of it as a sacred right, while you go for excluding all but them.

"But Brief is in a different position from you—and in degree much more consistent. He insists that all men—colored as well as white, and all women, too—white, black, and of every other hue—shall have the right to vote."

"But Brief is an Abolitionist and Woman's Rights man," said the Professor.

"Ah, and you are only a Democrat!" replied the Doctor. "But Brief says it is absurd for you to talk about democracy and equal rights, and that your pretence of being in favor of universal suffrage is a disreputable sham. He denies that sex or color are a righteous ground for depriving persons of their rights as human beings. And I perfectly agree with him."

"But surely," said the Professor, "you are not in favor of negroes and women being allowed to vote?"

"No," replied the Doctor, "not at all. But I agree with Brief, that negroes and women should not, because of their color or sex, be deprived of any of their rights as human beings, which they are competent to exercise; and I don't think their color or sex produces or betokens any such incapacity as ought—out of regard to their welfare or the public good—to exclude them.

"But then I differ from Brief about the nature of the right of suffrage. I hold it to be not a natural, but a civil right; not sacred, but merely prescriptive—one that rests in a grant from society, from the State—one that the people, the majority, may rightfully confer or withhold, extend, limit, and regulate at their pleasure,—not indeed in a merely capricious, unreasonable way, but as they shall truly judge best adapted to promote the great ends for which the State exists, for which governments exist—the maintenance of social justice and human welfare.

"The whole question of suffrage, therefore—its right and extent—is a question of expediency, what, namely, is best for the commonwealth. And I don't believe universal suffrage is best—neither in Brief's large sense of the word, nor in your narrower and improper use of it. I am sure the good of society requires all women should be excluded from voting; and as to men—though I would not exclude any one merely on account of his color, yet I would, as far as possible, make the qualifications of voters such as to include only those it would be best, for the good of the whole, to intrust with such a right—a right which (though not sacred in itself,) yet where granted involves duties that are sacred, and upon the wise and virtuous discharge of which the welfare of the nation depends."

" But how did you manage with Brief?" inquired the Professor.

"I asked him if he went for children having the right of suffrage, as well as as all grown-up persons of both sexes.

" He said no, he did not contend for that.

" I told him I wondered he did not. You go, said I, upon the principle that the State cannot, for any ends of its own, justly deprive any person of a right belonging to human persons as such?

" He said yes, he did.

" 'There is my daughter, Lilly, for instance,' I continued; 'she has done nothing against the laws; you would say the State has no more just right to put her to death or to make her work in a tread-mill —for any advantage to itself—than to do the same to me, or any other full-grown person innocent of crime?'

" 'True,' replied Brief, 'but the State gives you a right to control your daughter, and you, I presume, have no doubt but you may rightfully restrain her freedom.'

" 'Unquestionably,' I said, 'I have a certain right over her, not to be capriciously exercised, nor for my own own ends merely, but reasonably, within certain limits, in order that I may discharge my duty as a parent, and for the child's own good ; on the ground that her personality is imperfect, not yet so completely unfolded as that she can be safely left entirely to her own guidance. This right the State does not give me, but recognizes, and to a certain extent sustains ; and on the same ground the State assumes the right, because it is its duty, to control, directly or indirectly, all imperfect persons of mature age, the imbecile or insane.

"' But your suggestion has no force to establish your consistency, or to stop my argument. *Distinguemus distinguenda*—let us make all just distinctions. To regulate the exercise of a sacred right is a very different thing from prohibiting it altogether ; to restrain or limit it, for the good of those who are not mature persons enough to be capable of exercising it safely for themselves or for others, is one thing ; to take it entirely away, for mere State ends, from those who are capable of exercising it, is another and quite different thing. I may admit the justice of the one, without admitting the justice of the other.'

"' But in excluding children from voting,' said Brief, ' we go upon the ground that they are not capable, like full-grown persons, of exercising the right.'

"'Then I deny the matter of fact alleged,' said I. 'There is my boy Phil, twenty years old, he is just as competent as nine-tenths of the legal voters in the land; and there are thousands of the same age equally competent.'

"Brief admitted it was so, and thought it would be a just and good thing if twenty, or even eighteen, were made the legal age for voting.

"'But how are you going to stop there?' said I. 'There is Lilly, she is only fourteen; and there is Fred, he is twelve; yet you know, and I know, and everybody that knows them knows, that they are just as able to drop a ballot into the box as I am; as likely to do it out of an honest love for the commonwealth as most persons; and far more capable of doing it with a wise and intelligent judgment than multitudes who cast their votes; and there are tens of thousands of children equally as competent as they are.'

"'But,' said Brief, 'not all children are competent; so we have to draw a line and assume the fitness of those on one side, and the unfitness of those on the other.'

"'And assume what is not true,' said I. 'Is it not an established principle of justice, that the State shall not interfere with the sacred rights of persons except for good cause, established in each individual case?'

"'But we must have some practical rule in regard to suffrage,' said Brief.

"'And you can have no general rule,' said I, 'that will not either include some that are incompetent, and therefore, on your ground, have not the right, or exclude some that are competent, and therefore have the right to vote.

"'Don't you see, therefore, that you cannot get along on your ground? The only consistent conclusion is that suffrage is not a sacred right, but one that the State may, for its own ends, that is, for the good of the commonwealth, grant or deny, extend or limit, as it may judge best. It may, without injustice, establish a practical rule, although it should include some that are incompetent to vote, and exclude some that are competent. State machinery, like all other, is liable to fall short of theoretical perfection in its practical working. The ideally perfect can never be actually reached. All the State has to do is to do as well as it can. If it is practically best for the commonwealth to exclude from the exercise of suffrage, women and children, and negroes and foreigners, and one-half of the grown-up native-born white men, too, then it is right to do it, and the State, the people, if wise, should and will do it. And this is all there is to be said on the question of right in the matter.'"

CHAPTER XIX.

HARD AND DRY, PERHAPS—BUT GOING TO THE BOTTOM OF A SUBJECT IMMENSELY IMPORTANT TO BE UNDERSTOOD IN THIS COUNTRY.

"Government, my dear sir," said the Doctor, "is altogether a practical affair. That is best which works best, not that which you may think theoretically the best. But you have a vague notion that a democratic government is something intrinsically more just, and has a better moral right to exist, than a monarchical or aristocratic one. This is a groundless notion."

"But the people have the right of determining their form of government," said Professor Clare.

"True," replied the Doctor, "God has not prescribed any particular form, and we therefore infer that He has left the determination of it to society; and we infer, too, with equal right, that He does not care what the form is, provided it secure the ends for which the State exists, social justice and the public welfare. So far as the mere form is concerned, monarchy, aristocracy, democracy, have each an equal Divine sanction and right to exist; and the people may establish either of them, or any mixture or modification of them."

"The sovereignty, then, resides in the people," said the Professor.

"Yes," answered the Doctor, "necessarily, inherently, indefeasibly, and inalienably. But this sovereignty is not absolute and unbounded. It is limited by the very nature of the objects for which the State exists—the maintenance of the relations of right—the rights of every man as towards his fellows, and of his fellows as towards him: rights, I say, by which I mean whatever may be justly demanded by every man, and from every man in society—whatever is essential to his being and wellbeing as a man which he cannot, or ought not, or will not obtain singly, but only in, with, and through society. Wherever there are rights there is, or there should be, the power to enforce them. This is sovereignty—the sovereignty that resides in the people as a State—a sovereignty for right, but not for wrong. It is a sovereignty limited by duty, the duty of organizing and exercising the powers of the State to secure the best good of the people, so far as that lies within the sphere of the State. Any government that does this in any reasonably proximate way, is legitimate, no matter what its form, nor how it got established. I say, any government that does this in a reasonably proximate way; for you can no more expect to realize ideal perfection in government, than to realize the ideal figures of mathematics."

"But our immortal Declaration of Independence, lays it down that human governments derive their just powers from the consent of the governed," said the Professor.

"And like all such general positions," rejoined the Doctor, "it must be reasonably and not foolishly interpreted, otherwise the consequences become theoretically and practically troublesome.

"In the first place, as a doctrine on the origin and rightful ground of government, let us take care how we interpret it.

"The State, and there can be no State without a government of some sort, is as little the product of deliberate choice, as the result of chance or accidental discovery. It is no contrivance, no mutual insurance company or joint-stock association, nor any contract of parties creating what did not exist before. Men do not form a State and then go into it. They are born into it. It is something that exists wherever society exists—something that has always existed—something necessary and perpetual. Even Louis the Fourteenth, who said, 'I am the State,' said on his death-bed, 'I depart, but the State will endure forever.' It is something that gets itself formed, because there is a necessity for it, growing out of the necessity for men to live together in society.

"So originally with government, which is the organization and exercise of the powers of the State. Nothing can be more false and absurd than the theory which makes a 'social contract' the origin and rightful ground of government. Governments, in a right theoretical view, are not made, formed, constructed, put together, after a mere outward or mechanical fashion. They spring, grow, take form, get made of themselves, in a natural and living way. Spontaneous growth, from an inward principle, is the law of all organic life.

"Society, in its sovereign capacity, may indeed deliberately alter an existing or create a new form of government; but the State, with some form of government, must have pre-existed, to render this possible. In point of fact, governments are seldom the result of deliberate adoption. They are mostly the product of spontaneous growth, or of the necessity of circumstances, and none the worse, in the latter case, if the necessity be an internal one. Foreign force and imposition apart, the fact that a government exists and maintains itself in the exercise of the supreme powers of the State, is, generally speaking, the sufficient consent of the governed—by governed meaning the nation in its sovereign capacity. No formal consent is necessary. The consent is something that may be rightfully assumed.

"But, perhaps, in the next place, by the consent of the governed, you do not mean the formal, nor even the implicit and assumed consent of the nation, but the consent, express or tacit, of the individuals that compose it? I should not wonder if this were your notion."

"It is something like it, I confess," said the Professor.

"But thus understood," said the Doctor, "your immortal Declaration would express something as absurdly false as can well be conceived.

"For does the sovereignty of the people reside in the individuals that compose the nation—distinctly, separately and independently in each? If so, then either it is complete and entire in each;

each individual is the sovereign, or one of the sovereigns, according to a phrase we often hear, so that the sovereignty of the State is merely a collective word to express the total number or aggregation of these distinct, separate and independent sovereignties.

"Or else it is fractionally in each; each possesses distinctly, separately and independently, a fractional part—so that the one whole and complete sovereignty of the people is composed or constituted by the addition of these distinct, separate and independent fractions of sovereignty.

"But neither view can hold. Falsehood and absurdity either way.

"You might as truly and wisely say that your hands or feet, your fingers or toes, every several muscle and nerve of your body, possesses each a distinct, separate and independent life and living power of action and motion; or that a fractional part of the life and power of the body resides distinctly, separately and independently in each several member and organ.

"The sovereignty of the people, complete, entire and undivided, resides in the people, as one whole body, and not at all in the individual. Sovereignty is not an attribute of individuals. It is impossible it should be. The sovereignty of the State is that which, within its sphere, has at once the supreme right and power in and of itself, to govern, to make its will valid and irresistibly effectual. This no individual can possess. No despot that ever lived, not the most absolute wielder of the supreme powers of the State, ever did possess it. Louis the Fourteenth, who called himself the State, was never the sovereign of France in the high sense of the word, because he never was the State, nor could be. He never possessed the sovereignty of France—never possessed nor exercised in his sole person, the right and power, in and of himself, to make his own will irresistibly valid. His power, great as it was, stood in the consent of the people, not indeed formally and individually expressed, but in their consent, or it could not have stood at all; but he was more or less checked in the absolute despotic exercise of it in many ways—by public opinion, by old maxims, laws and institutions of the State.

"The sovereignty, then, is neither inherent in the members of a State, as individuals—nor does the possession of political rights and the exercise of political power by individuals—all, many, or one, makes no difference—vest the sovereignty in the individual, making him wholly or fractionally a sovereign.

"The notion, therefore, of the necessity of the 'consent of the governed,' in their individual capacity, going upon the idea that the sovereignty of the State, or any share of it, is possessed by the members of the State, as individuals—and the notion can go upon no other idea—is one that cannot stand. It is as groundless as the idea it goes upon.

"Besides: your immortal Declaration is universal in its terms. It should be so, on the principle you adopt; for if it hold at all, it must hold of all. Let us see where we get. There are, for instance, a great many malcontents among us, who do not consent to our Constitution, but would rather overthrow it; some in the name of liberty and the sacred rights of man, some in the name of slavery and the sacred right of property in man. Are such persons, therefore, absolved from allegiance to it, or has our government no just power over them?"

"But the consent of the majority, I suppose, is meant," said the Professor.

"Well," rejoined the Doctor, "that is giving up the proposition in its terms, as implying the individual consent of all the governed. So far so good. But to say that human governments derive their just powers from the consent of the majority of the governed, whether of all the individuals in the State, or of a part of them, (those, namely, who are voters,) is equally a false interpretation of your immortal Declaration. The just powers of a government stand only in the consent of the body in which the sovereignty inherently resides. There is no inherent sovereignty in a majority any more than in a minority, either as individuals or as a body. The sovereignty, as I have said, is in the people of the State, as one whole body. It is a sovereignty of which the people cannot divest themselves. They may indeed delegate the practical exercise of the powers of the State, at their pleasure and during their pleasure, to one, to many, or to all, of the members of the State— may delegate, that is, all they can delegate, with or without conditions and limitations, as they may choose. In a democratic, or in a mixed republican State, where popular suffrage prevails, the sovereign consent of the people may find expression, their sovereign will may get practical validity, through the action of all the voters and the concurrence of a majority of them ; only you must remember that the action of the majority is taken as decisive of any question submitted to suffrage, not because of any inherent exclusive right in the majority to be the decisive organ of the sovereign, any more than to be the sovereign itself, but simply from the necessity of having a decision, and because it is assumed to be, on the whole, the wisest and most expedient way of getting it, though it may happen in many cases that the actual decision is very far from being the wisest and best.

" You must distinguish then between the sovereign and its representative—between the power that delegates and the authority that is delegated. In governments where the constitution and the administration of the powers of the State depend primarily upon the action of a majority, both its action and that of all the public functionaries created by it, is taken and held to be not their action, but that of the sovereign State. It runs in the name of the people, and is so recited in all official forms. It is, for instance, ' The People of the State of New York,' that is said to enact, judge, and execute, through them. Their authority is not imperial, but only ministerial. The only imperial power is that of the People of the State.

" You must remember, too, that the majority, acting as the representative of the sovereign State, cannot rightfully exercise its delegated authority in any arbitrary or absolute way. The sovereign State itself has imperial power only within its sphere and for its just ends. It cannot delegate what it does not possess. The State is a moral person; it has of right no sovereign power to do wrong, and it can confer no such power. It has no just right to have its own will and way at all events and in any way; and it can invest no majority acting in its name and behalf with any such right. The rightful powers of a majority are restrained by all the limitations by which the sovereignty of the people is restrained. The stream cannot rise higher than the source from which it springs.

"And here we touch upon the great danger in all governments—the danger of absolutism. All power is liable to abuse. Absolute power is safe only in the hands of God. It is always dangerous in human hands, whether lodged in one, in a few, or in the majority. Yet public power inevitably tends to absolutism. But democratic absolutism is as dangerous as monarchical—more so in some respects; and it is less easily got rid of, when it becomes intolerable. It is possible to cut off the head of a single tyrant, but who is to cut off the million heads of a tyrannical majority?

"Democratic power has its flatterers, equally

with monarchical. Demagogues are the courtiers of the majority. The sense of moral responsibility is comparatively little felt by men acting in a mass—especially if irritated by opposition, as they are prone to be, or excited by passion, as they are very liable to be. The absolute will of a single despot is restrained by many necessities and limitations, moral and circumstantial. His power cannot stand solely in himself; it must support itself on something without, on opinion. He is compelled to consider whether he can effect what he wishes. Louis Napoleon's imperial throne could not stand for a day, if it had nothing to rest upon but his hundred and seventy-five thousand bayonets. But what is there to restrain a majority bent on having its own way? It makes its own opinion, and there is no outside power able to resist its will.

"Many persons talk as if there was no other absolutism than monarchical. This is a mistake. The Athenian government became a democratic absolutism. So did the French at one time. So may any other. And there are no atrocities of tyranny perpetrated by single despots, but democratic despotism has equalled or surpassed them. Pharaoh put the male infants of the Hebrews to death, to prevent the increase of that people; the Spartans were wont to kill the Helots, 'as many' (the historian says) 'as was necessary,' whenever they found their numbers inconveniently large. The massacre of St. Bartholomew's finds its prototype in the murder of the minority by the Corcyrean majority. Some old tyrant (I forget his name) put a man to death who dreamed he had slain the tyrant, and was foolish enough to tell his dream. But the French tribunals at one time beat that; they cut off old women's heads, for 'suspicion of *incivisme*,' suspicion of not being inwardly pleased with the bloody doings of the majority! I doubt if the records of monarchical despotism can show any thing equal to that.

"Do not infer from this that I am in favor of monarchical absolutism. I would have none of any sort. I mean only to enforce the necessity of guarding against the dangerous tendency to democratic absolutism. Let the majority get a habit of feeling that they are the people—that they have the right to do whatever they like, and to treat the minority as if not belonging to the people—that he who opposes a monarchical absolutism is a hero, and, if he falls, a martyr in a sacred cause, but he who opposes the absolutism of a majority, is a criminal, who may rightfully be crushed by the sovereign power he opposes; let such sentiments come to prevail, and what will there be but the worst of all tyrannies, the tyranny of an irresponsible, irresistible majority? What force, then, in laws and constitutions?

"I do not say we have come to this, or are coming. But is there not reason enough, in human nature, in the quality of power to delight in itself; to grow and strengthen itself; to impose upon its own conscience, with a notion of its inherent right; to be irritated at opposition, and so become self-willed and unjust; in all this, and in the pernicious influence of demagogue courtiers, their arts and flatteries, is there not reason enough for apprehension of what may come in the future? Are there no tokens of the existence of such false and dangerous sentiments? Are there no symptoms of their increase and spread?

"The more popular rights, the more duties, and the more need of wisdom and goodness in the people."

CHAPTER XX.

VERY SHORT, PERHAPS UNPALATABLE—YET, IF TRUE, OUGHT NOT TO GIVE OFFENCE TO ANY GOOD MAN.

"But, perhaps, husband, you have not the faith you should have in the virtue of the people," said Mrs. Oldham. She had been listening in silence until now.

"I have all proper respect for the virtue of the people," replied the Doctor. "I believe the great mass of them have virtue enough to follow their private callings, for the most part, with tolerable honesty—many of them with exemplary uprightness. The great mass of the people, especially 'off the pavements,' as an eminent statesman and friend of mine says, have political virtue enough to wish the country to be rightly and uprightly governed. But their virtue doesn't prevent their being tools in the hands of political managers."

"But who are they?"

"Very different men, my dear, from those of the earlier and better times. Sixty years ago men like John Jay—a name synonymous with every thing great and good—statesmanly wisdom, pure patriotism, unsullied honor, incorruptible integrity, had an influence in public affairs, and on the politics of the State, which such men do not have now."

"But of what sort are the managers nowadays?"

"Professor Clare knows, my dear. Are they such men as John Jay, Professor?"

"No, I must confess they are not," said he.

"But what is their character?" persisted Mrs. Oldham.

"You have no personal acquaintance with such men; I trust you will never have; and it is hard to make you comprehend precisely the species. But in general you may understand that they are men of small private and less public virtue. If we look to the case of your native city below, I should say the individual managers are for the most part men your father would not have liked to shake hands or walk the streets with. There was a time, in his day, when a De Witt Clinton could be be mayor for twelve years, and Richard Varick for I don't know how many."

"But could not such men have the office nowadays, if they would take it?"

"No, my dear, not a chance for it, unless in some extraordinary combined reaction of the property-holders and decent and respectable people of all parties, after some stupendously profligate and corrupt administration, it might be possible to put an able and good man in for once. But for the most part it is necessary to success that a man renounce integrity and honor; put himself into the hands of party politicians; give pledges of jobs, contracts and plunder to men who make corruption a trade, buying up at the highest price the suffrages and fists of the affiliated vice and ruffianism, that holds the balance of power.

"No, my dear wife, New York is ruled nowadays by such men as—rule it.

"How far the same thing is true elsewhere and throughout the country, is more than would be pleasant for you to know.

"So much for the political virtue of the people. Really I do not think there is any too much of it, not enough, I am afraid, for us to get on in the best way. But we shall get on after a fashion for some time, I make no doubt. But if we keep on as we are now going, there will come a time when we shall not get on at all; things will rush down, perhaps, in some memorably disastrous way, and amidst anarchic storms and darkness, get righted again in some fashion, as best it can, for another start. The old story over again. But I think not in our time, wife. Possibly we may grow better before it gets to that."

"Oh, I hope we may, husband."

"It is a Christian wish, wife, in which I heartily join."

CHAPTER XXI.

ALSO SHORT—NOT WITHOUT INTEREST FOR SOME MINDS—BUT LIKELY TO DISPLEASE TWO SORTS OF READERS AND TO SHOCK ONE OF THEM.

"But there is our system of public instruction," said the Professor; "our common schools, primary and higher, with our admirable school libraries;—there is something to give us hope for a better future."

"All very well, and much to be rejoiced in," returned the Doctor, "but not enough in themselves to make private or public virtue sure. Knowledge is a power for evil as well as for good.

"You remind me of something that happened a little while ago in town. I was in the book repository of one of the most eminent publishing houses of the country, passing down the long length of that vast hall, with its two rows of handsome columns supporting the ceiling, and looking at the immense piles of books—eighty thousand volumes—ordered by the State of Ohio for their public school libraries—lying there to be made ready for transportation—when the head of the house, who was walking with me, remarked that Mr. Cobden, the celebrated member of the British Parliament, then on a visit to this country, was there a few days before, and, looking at the books, said to him : 'Ah, Mr. A———, there is the bulwark of your institutions.'

"Ah, Mr. A———," said I, "why didn't you tell him the Evil One knows ten times as much as there is in all the books in your store, and it doesn't make him good at all ? "

"But are you sure Mr. Cobden believes there is any Evil One ? " said Professor Clare.

"That makes no difference to the argument," replied the Doctor.

"But you believe there is one ? " said the Professor.

"Well, if there be," said the Doctor, "he is God's creature—for I don't believe in an infinite and self-existent Evil One—and so I hope God will be able to reclaim him to goodness, as I am sure His nature would lead Him to wish to do. But I am quite sure no amount of 'useful knowledge' will ever make him good."

"O husband, why do you speak in such a way? Mrs. Shafton was scandalized the other day by what you said."

"What was it?"

"Something about the Evil One, much like what you have just now said."

"What, my charitable wish for his conversion?"

"Yes, you quite shocked her."

"Then she needed to be shocked. A person who is shocked at the mere suggestion of a benevolent wish, for the restoration to goodness and blessedness, of one of the highest order of God's spiritual creatures, ought to be shocked a number of times—if only it would do any good."

"But she supposed you meant he would be restored."

"That is not my fault. I didn't say any such thing; and a person ought to have a double galvanic shock, for not distinguishing between the suggestion of a charitable wish and a positive belief on the subject—if it would quicken the faculty of distinguishing just distinctions. Which is the most shocking, the most contradictory to the natural and necessary impulse of the best and most gracious feelings of the benevolent heart, to wish the evil and wretched may continue eternally evil and wretched, or to wish they may become good and blessed? It seems to me the former is far the most shocking of the two."

"But you don't believe he will be restored?"

"No, though it has been the belief of many great and godly men and doctors of the church, from the time of Origen to the present day. But I have no doctrine on the subject, whatever I may wish or hope. I don't know but he will continue forever evil; and if so he must be forever wretched. That is a law of the spiritual universe, which the Almighty cannot abrogate if He would, and ought not if He could.

"But this I do know: that it lies in the very necessity of God's essential Goodness—His Loving Holiness and Holy Lovingness—that He should desire and—as far as in Him lies—secure the goodness, and thereby the blessedness, of all His spiritual creatures. He would not otherwise be God. He would become—I speak it in no irreverent spirit—the Infinite Evil One. This I know by the necessity of the reason He has given me.

"I know, too, as a matter of fact, that His love is not confined to the good. It embraces the sinful race of man. He has shown it in some very wonderful methods for our restoration. And I see no reason in the nature of superhuman sinful spirits, if such there are—the Bible says there are, and it is nothing strange there should be—why they should be excluded from the sphere of God's reclaiming love. He is the Father of their spirits as much as of ours. They are His children as much as we are. They must have been, like us, originally pure and good—for God made them, and higher and brighter, we are told, in order and endowment than our race. They fell from goodness and bliss in the same way as we did, in spite of the good and gracious spirit of God in them to help them keep right, —fell through abuse of their freedom, that awful endowment, without which there could be no moral universe."

"But, husband, the Bible seems to say that in point of fact they will continue forever evil and wretched."

"It may be so; God cannot *force* them to become good any more than us; but we must believe in Him as doing all He can for their restoration. They may be forever evil and so forever wretched, because they can resist all God's love and grace drawing them to goodness. This is the only way we can reconcile such a sad fate with the idea of a proper moral universe, the only way to have a good God and common sense in our theology.

"But the thought of Eternal Evil in the spiritual universe of the Infinite, Holy, Loving All-Father, is one I do not like to entertain. The thought that it will be so through defect of any thing He can do to prevent it is monstrous. The thought that it will be so through any eternal purpose or agency of His is abominable. It is not the 'enmity of the carnal heart,' as some folks say, that resists it; it is the voice of God in the universal reason and conscience revolting against the atrocious doctrine. I would rather be an Atheist than hold it.

"Is it not better, more congruous with every dictate of a good and benevolent heart, to hope that in some way, yet unknown to us, Evil will go down, vanquished, absorbed, extinguished and destroyed by the all-conquering power of Infinite Love? How great its resources may be, without doing violence to spiritual freedom, who can tell?"

I have already, at the outset of this work, apprised the reader that the Doctor would be likely to say a good many things not perfectly acceptable to everybody, and some perhaps offensive to many persons, including all the Pharisees, Sadducees and Herodians, who, as well as some of quite a different and better sort, are all likely to be displeased with this chapter.

I do not hold myself responsible for all the Doctor's utterances. My business is to record his talk. At the same time I would not set down any thing which I did not think would, on the whole, be approved by all courteous, candid, intelligent, discriminating, thoughtful and judicious readers, and such I take it are all who read, and certainly all who like this book.

CHAPTER XXII.

THE DOCTOR AT A WOMAN'S RIGHTS CONVENTION—WHAT HE DID NOT SAY THERE, BUT WOULD HAVE SAID IF HE HAD SAID ANY THING.

Mrs. OLDHAM was sitting one evening listening in her placid way to something she did not take much interest in, which Professor Clare was reading to the Doctor out of a newspaper he had brought with him when he came in, employing herself the while with one of those elegant industries which occupy the hands of women without absorbing their attention.

There is a fashion, I observe, in these things; and her work was of a sort I perceive to have become very fashionable of late—the netting of soft wools into various articles for women's heads and shoulders, and even into cloaks and large shawls or blankets—*Afghans,* Lilly says they call them—to be worn as a protection against dust in summer drives. Very beautiful fabrics, too, many of them are, from their rich harmony of manifold bright colors, and so fleecy and light withal, that there is not the least feeling of weight in wearing them.

I have often heard it said it was a pity that gentlemen have not some nice occupation for their hands, too, during the hours they pass with the women in the family reunion, or in the small social gathering; for that it makes the men look so loutish to be sitting idly by, or only wagging their tongues, while the women's nimble fingers are producing such pretty and useful results, all the time their tongues are running on in the most agreeable way.

But I could never agree with this opinion. It seems to me this occupation of the hands at such times is something exclusively feminine, and marking very fitly a distinction between men and women I lay the greatest stress upon the observance of. Of course I am not speaking in the spirit of an American savage, nor of the drudgeries of labor; and so, Miss Amanda Rose, your sweet earnest face need not flush with the sacred fire of holy displeasure. I intend nothing derogatory to your lovely sex. On the contrary, my opinion is grounded in a sentiment of genuine reverence for all that is most truly womanly, and therefore most to be reverenced in woman. And I am happy to have the Doctor's wife on my side in this matter. For I asked her how she liked the notion of such parlor occupations for men's fingers. She said—not at all ; she would be ashamed to see them, it would look so unmanly ; she would rather see the men twiddling their fingers the whole evening without saying a word.

"Ah, my dear," said the Doctor, "you are not one of the strong-minded women. You should have attended the Woman's Rights Convention that was held here last week. You might have been converted by the beautiful eloquence of those female apostles. You might have caught the spirit of sublime devotion with which they declared their resolution never to give over demanding the sacred right of making men of themselves, and their readiness, if need be, ' to lay themselves '—in their own exalted language—' on the altar of sacrifice ' for the holy cause."

"I am glad I did not go to see women behaving in such an unwomanly way," said Mrs. Oldham. "I should have been ashamed at the sight ; and I certainly was ashamed of you for countenancing them by your presence, as you did.

"Do you know," she continued, addressing Professor Clare, "that my husband was there the whole time? He came home during their recess, and could talk of nothing but the beautiful faces of some of those women, and the beautiful language and way of speaking of all of them. He went back without his dinner—we dine late, you know—because he would not miss the afternoon speeches; and was in a hurry for his tea at night, that he might attend their last session. I was seriously afraid he was going to catch the infection of their doctrines; in fact I expected nothing but he would—with the zeal of a new convert—bring home with him the strong-minded President, and the chief preacher, and certainly the beautiful young orator, Miss Paulina Paul, who did not believe in St. Paul, but whose loveliness—of *mind*—filled him —my husband, I mean, not St. Paul—with such rapt admiration. Think of my having to act the part of Martha and of Mary both to such exalted guests—to serve them, and at the same time to sit at their feet, if peradventure I might be also converted to a disciple, and perhaps to an apostle, for that I suppose is what my husband would have hoped for."

" Ah, wife, I don't doubt you would have made a charming apostle of Woman's Rights—perhaps all the better for having such a gift for inventing facts, as you have just shown. But I had rather have you as you are. I could not get along without you at home, and it would be out of the question my accompanying you on your apostolic travels. All the while the chief preacher, the Reverend Mrs. Black Brown, was talking, I could not help thinking with pity of her husband, and how lonely and dreary he must find his home, after being hard at work all day among his patients, while she is always away on those missionary excursions, spreading the Gospel of Woman's Rights. I don't think apostles of either sex ought to be married, and that, I presume, is the reason why I listened with so much more pleasure to the lovely Paulina Paul, and even to the hard-faced Margaret St. Anthony, than to the fervent Mrs. Black Brown. I was not disturbed in their case by any compassionate thoughts of pining babies and forlorn husbands. But then Dr. Black Brown has no reason to complain; for his wife—I ought rather to say his partner—told me she made it a condition of entering into the partnership, that he should stay at home and take care of the children, leaving her at liberty to go whenever and wherever she pleased, in the fulfilment of her great mission."

"But you did attend the Convention?" said the Professor.

"Yes," replied the Doctor, "my wife is right as to that. In this age of great movements of social reform, I think it quite proper for those who have any function of public instruction by speech or pen, to make themselves acquainted with the way in which these modern notions are held in the minds of the leaders. So I went to the place of meeting, and was standing on the steps when the President, Miss Margaret St. Anthony, came up; and a person with whom I was talking presented me to her, without waiting to learn if it would be mutually agreeable. She said she hoped I would go in and take part in the discussions they were about to engage in.

"I told her I could not think of debating such questions with the women."

"'Ah,' said she, 'you don't think us women worthy of being argued with?'

"'I don't indeed think,' said I, 'that the logical faculty is so pre-eminently the gift of women in general, as that of quick intuitional insight, and the latter, it seems to me, is a finer one than the merely logical discursive faculty—at all events a different one, and the characteristic endowment of women.'

"'But how do you know,' said she, 'we

should not evince an equal degree of logical power, if we had the same advantages of training as the men.'

"'Very possibly,' said I, 'and in many instances undoubtedly in a higher degree than most men. But I think there is a sex in souls as well as in bodies.'

"'We do not deny that,' was her reply; 'but should woman on that account be deprived of her rights?'

"'By no means,' I answered; 'most certainly not of any sacred rights, belonging to human persons as such, nor of your special rights as women, to be good daughters, sisters, wives, mothers, housewives, mistresses and friends; and as to all other rights, I don't know any objection to your having as many of them as you want, if it don't unsex you, and spoil you for being the particular sort of divine thing you were Divinely made to be. I don't know as you care for the right of bearing arms, running with the fire engines, holding the plough, going on whaling voyages, and such like—and if you do, I don't know as there is any thing to hinder your enjoyment of them, except your inability to discharge them to any good purpose. But there is one right in particular we men have, I hardly dare ask whether you desire to possess it.'

"'What is it?'

"'The right of making fools of ourselves.'

"'Ah, you think we women are not deprived of that right,' said she.

"By this time the hour for opening the Convention had come, and she went in to preside.

"My wife is partly right in what she says of the impression they produced on my mind; for it was to me a very striking and curious sight to see those women, most of them quite young, many of them very pretty, and all of them very bright-minded, making themselves foolish, which is certainly one of the rights they enjoy equally with us men. And such beautiful writers and speakers were they, and mistresses (masters if they prefer) of such a clear, pure English style, and such true eloquence of speech—putting most men to shame in these respects, and with such ingenious sophistries did they blend the true and the false together, and beg the very questions to be proved—unconsciously I am bound to think, for they did it with such apparent good faith and simple earnestness of conviction—that I could not but think it would go hard but they would upset the world, were it not that the Good Lord had had the making of it.

"When the talking was all over, and the Convention dissolved, as I was passing out, the chief preacher asked me if I was in any degree converted by what I had heard.

"'Not the least in the world,' said I; 'all you and your sister apostles have so beautifully and eloquently said, has made no more impression upon my judgment than the little hail drops on the windows; for I see the principles you go upon are very false and very bad.'

"'But why,' said she, 'did you not express your views in the Convention? We repeatedly invited those who did not think with us to speak their thoughts freely.'

"'True,' I replied, 'but you took care not to give them the least chance to do so. You did not wait so much as one-quarter of a minute in any instance, before some one of your own number began talking again.'"

"But, surely, husband, you would not have spoken there, even if they had given you a chance?" said Mrs. Oldham.

"Certainly not, my dear; nothing could have induced me to open my mouth in such an assembly; and even if I had been otherwise disposed to do so, I should have been deterred by the fear of exposing myself to vulgar abuse by way of answer,

—I don't mean from the women in women's clothes that were there, certainly not from the lovely Paulina Paul, but from one or both of two speakers who sat on the platform in men's clothes, one of whom spoke very abusively of St. Paul. If a tailor be but the ninth part of a man, according to the old saying—I don't say I believe it—what fraction of a man must a male human being be who goes about to these Woman's Rights meetings, under the leadership of the strong-minded Margaret St. Anthony? I certainly feel no contempt for the St. Anthony, though I don't admire her person or her principles; but for such amphibious animals as those—neither men nor women—my feelings are not altogether of the most respectful sort."

"But what would you have said, if you had been disposed to give them a serious homily?" inquired the Professor.

"Well," said the Doctor, "I should have said something on this wise:

"Dearly beloved sisters—I have heard many things here to-day that are true enough—though nothing new in them—and reasonable enough, and good enough, mixed up with a great many things that are not true at all, nor reasonable, nor good.

"You ought undoubtedly to have a chance to

be well educated as women, equal to that which the men have for being educated as men.

"I agree with you also in wishing there were a greater number of respectable and well-paid feminine industries, for those women who are obliged to earn their own livelihood.

"There is room, too, perhaps, for some improvements in the legal relations of women—particularly to prevent drunken husbands from wasting property that is necessary for the support of their families.

"As to all these things, you either already have them, or can have them, and nobody objects to your having them.

"But as to the rest, the principles you go upon are all mere falsehood and delusion, and the notions you propound as to what you would do and have done, are all nonsense and foolishness—springing, I fear, from sheer unwomanly vanity, pride, and naughtiness of heart; and if they were carried fully out—which I thank God is impossible in the very constitution of things—they would entirely subvert God's ordinations in the world, and work the greatest imaginable mischief; spoil you for being good women, only to make bad men of you; destroy all true domestic life, and finally extinguish the human race.

"For God has made you to be women, just as he has made men to be men. Both are human beings, and so far alike. But there are two sorts of human beings—human men and human women —different from each other with a difference running through their whole organization, physical, physiological, mental and moral—a difference in bones, muscles, quality of predominant blood, nervous system, and temperament; in the degree and quality and combination of gifts, aptitudes, bents, capacities, affections, and dispositions, of mind, heart, and soul. I speak, of course, of men and women according to the idea and type after which God made them; I speak of them as they were meant to be, and for the most part are, and for the most part will continue to be, in spite of the misguided attempts of such exceptional women, and exceptional men, as some I see here to-day.

"This difference—this constitutional and inextinguishable difference—is nothing derogatory to you. The question about the equality of the sexes is as absurd as the question whether the whiteness of a lily is equal to the fragrance of a rose. They are things not to be compared in such a way. You might as well think the difference of sexual organization derogatory to you, as to think so of the difference in mind, heart and soul. It implies no inferiority in rank, dignity, or worth. The perfection of each is in being true to the law of their being—woman to the idea of womanhood, man to the idea of manhood. In this respect only can woman be equal to man, or man equal to woman—equal in dignity and worth; and this is the only equality that either of us should strive after.

"Besides, man and woman are made for each other. Each needs the other, and neither is perfect without the other. It is only when man and woman are united that the perfection of either is realized. This is possible only through the opposite qualities of each. Electrical forces of the same sort repel each other—there is mutual attraction only between opposite poles. It is equally so in the spiritual world. Make men women or women men, and there can be no true union. It is only womanly women and manly men that can become truly one.

"The characteristic qualities of woman—when true to the type of her being—her delicacy, modesty, reserve, and chastity in thought and feeling, word and action—her sweetness, gentleness, patience, sympathy, tenderness, dependence, devotion; her sensibility to beauty and grace, order, fitness and propriety in speech, dress, behavior, every thing; her intellectual faculties—more receptive than productive—thought resting more on feeling than feeling on thought—making her more susceptible of culture and refinement than apt for grasping the abstruse and rugged in science and practical life; all these are her charms for man, through which man gets unspeakable good to his own nature; while man's harder texture in body and mind—his strength, courage, self-reliance, his grasp, force, and productive power in the world of thought and action, draw woman to him. Thus each finds in the other what each one needs. The womanly woman feels herself strong and brave when she leans on man, and man's manly courage grows stouter, and at the same time the rugged hardness of his nature is softened by tender reverence, as with one arm he supports and with the other protects the gentle one clinging to his side. In every thing, in short, in which they are made different, it is that each may find their proper counterpart in the other. They are made different in order that they may become one. Out of this very difference springs the closest and richest union—the union of mutual love, whereof marriage is the outward representation. Only in this true married union, and in the home of love that builds itself up out of it, can the fulness and perfection of the individual life, dignity, and worth of each be found and realized.

"In this union your part and lot is fixed and made necessary by a wisdom greater than yours. God has made you to be wives and mothers, just as He has made men to be husbands and fathers. All talk about sameness of rights is absurd. You cannot have the rights of husbands and fathers, because you cannot discharge the duties of husbands and fathers. The husband is the head of the family, the wife his help-meet. This comes of itself naturally in every true union of love between a manly man and a womanly woman. It is the dignity and worth and happiness of both, notwithstanding the grandiloquent nonsense of your chief preacher, who declares 'the individual life problem of a human soul is not solvable, if any one lives to be the help of another;' nonsense which might be pernicious, but that He who said, 'it is not good for man to be alone, I will make him a *help-meet* for him,' is stronger in woman's nature than the nonsense that contradicts His wise plan.

"Home, then, the Home of Love, is the sacred sphere of woman's noblest activities, her duties and her joys. Abroad, indeed, in the social circle, she has her place, as a woman, to please and be pleased, to brighten and adorn, to do good and to get good. But in the sacred intimacies of home is the centre of her life. While the husband watches over, protects, provides, engages in the outward activities on which the welfare of the family depends, the duties of his calling and those which the public safety and the public weal impose, the loving wife and mother presides within, with gracious and graceful assiduities, caring for the comfort, health and welfare of all, nurturing the children in goodness, affection, reverence, duty, truth, honor, love of country and of God. She is the good genius of the house, through whose benignant skill all things get well ordered, take a bright and cheerful look, and the air of the home becomes full of peace and the perfume of flowers. She has a fairy art, born only of love, that throws a nameless charm over the homeliest things in the loving eyes that see, and the loving hearts that feel her to be the centre of the household life, its grace and graciousness—instinctively see and feel it, even though the faculty to analyze and reflect upon it be not unfolded. 'Her children rise up and call her blessed, and her husband he praiseth her.' Thus in loving and being loved, she finds the fulness of her life.

"This is home as I find it; for there is a true woman and a loving wife and mother in my home.

"Such is woman's noble and blessed destination to bring man and herself back to Eden again.

"But you would spoil it all with your foolish unwomanly notions. You know not what mischief you are about. You would break out from home, neglect your proper work in life—which you alone can do—to engage in what is not your work, and what you cannot do. You clamor for Woman's Rights, forgetting that you enjoy all the most sacred rights you can have—those that spring from sacred duties—the right to be good wives and mothers. You renounce the true rights of woman, to grasp at those you were not made for and cannot have. What you really clamor for is the right to make men of yourselves. But you are no more fitted for the social, civil, and public functions of men than you are for those of husbands and fathers; and the thought of your attempting the one, is scarcely less unnatural and monstrous, than that of the other; certainly it is equally contrary to the constitution of your nature, and to God's order of things therein established; it would only work mischief and ruin to yourselves, to the commonwealth, and to society in all its interests and relations.

"You demand a change in the legal relations of husband and wife. Because there are some bad husbands, as well as bad wives, you would have laws made, which, I am sure, would tend to the great increase of both. Bad husbands are the exceptions. The laws go—as they should do—upon this supposition. You demand that they shall go upon the assumption of the contrary. Not only so, but you would subvert the very principle of our laws. They go upon the principle that marriage is a sacred union of mind, soul and heart, as well as of bodies—a union with one head, and that the man—in which there can of right be no conflicting interests. This principle is grounded in the ordination of God as expressed in the constitution of man's and woman's nature, recognized by reason, and plainly taught in the Christian religion. You would have them go upon the principle that marriage is a contract of selfish convenience—a two-headed partnership, in which the separate interests of the parties, or rather your separate interests, which are all you seem to care for, shall be jealously secured.

"What would be the effect? Why, as far as it had any, it would give occasion, and scope, and temptation to a thousand-fold more violations of sacred duty, and more domestic mischiefs and miseries than it would prevent.

"You insist on the right of engaging in all the industrial and professional callings and employments of men—or such of them as you may choose.

"Well, I don't know as any thing stands in the way of this but public opinion—except, in the matter of becoming public ministers of religion, there are some remarkable words of St. Paul, commonly understood as speaking by Divine direction, which bear rather hard upon the self-ordained Reverend Mrs. Black Brown. But she has braved St. Paul and public opinion both. You can all do the same. Perhaps you can change the public opinion. I rather think not. But you can brave it. You can enter on any career of activity now considered as exclusively within man's proper sphere—for I take it, of course, it is only in regard to such that you have any quarrel with public opinion. But with what result? You cannot succeed. You could not do the work in competition with man, if all the opinion in the world gave you an equal chance. The world has a way of its own in such things. It will employ and pay those who do the world's work best. Perhaps you might make the men abstain from competition, or stay at home and take care of the house and nurse babies, to give you a clear field. This is doubtful. The great odds are you would unsex yourselves to little purpose—spoil yourselves for being good women only to make unsuccessful men of yourselves.

"But to cap the climax of your foolishness, you insist upon women having the same political rights as men. Not contented with being represented at the polls by your fathers, brothers, husbands, and all other men that vote, you insist on going there in person, as the sacred right of woman, short of which nothing will content you; though if suffrage were a sacred right, which it is not, there are thousands of young women and girls under twenty-one, equally capable of voting as you are, who might protest against being represented at the polls by you, and challenge the equal right of going there with you to cast their votes. But to leave them out of view—you demand that the Constitution of the State shall be so altered as to give you the same right of suffrage as the men enjoy. You demand also the same right to hold political offices, and discharge the public functions of the State. This is what you ask for in the memorial to the Legislature, you have passed about for signatures here to-day.

"Suppose you gain your end?

"What then?

"Either: the women would not avail themselves of their new rights—unless a few such exceptional women as some here now; and so nothing or but little would come of it.

"Or, else: they would—which is what you desire and contemplate.

"Suppose, then, all the women in the land to enter into politics, seek public offices, take sides in party conflicts, and throng the polls with the men.

"I pass over the scenes in the legislative halls, and in the courts, which the reporters for the press might have to portray; the nurseries added to the committee-rooms of the legislative halls and jury rooms of the courts; and the ludicrous interruptions of public business and the course of justice, through mistaken reckoning of time or premature effects of fatigue and public cares—all which are possibilities in the case of women. I pass over the spectacles likely to be presented at the polls—particularly in the great towns where now the majority of the votes are cast, especially in times when party feeling runs high, as it does in nearly all elections now—pure and gentle and delicate women—if such could be supposed to go there, and that is what you would have them do—jostled and hustled among rival crowds of brutal and ruffianly men, augmented by crowds of rival women of their own social standing and degree. I pass over also the possible neglect of the special duties of wives and mothers, and the moral injury to the children, the household discomforts and domestic disunion that might thence ensue. I pass over all this, and lay no stress upon it; for I know all that can be said in reply. I put it out of sight, because there is a deeper and more thoughtful view I would have you take.

"When you enter into politics and public life, you step out of your proper sphere, and you cannot do this without mischief to yourselves, to man, and to the interests of the State. Woman's relation to the State is through the family and the society of private life. Here is the sphere in which she is to serve her country. Here lies her influence—and influence is woman's true power—an influence graceful and gracious, beautiful and salutary—imbuing the minds of children with lofty and generous sentiments, honor, justice and love of country, and keeping such sentiments alive and warm in the hearts of husbands, fathers, brothers, and all within her social circle—humanizing, softening, refining and ennobling the manners, tempers, and whole social life of man—and especially mediating between conflicting elements, smoothing the asperities and allaying the animosities of party spirit among men whose interests or sense of public duty put them in opposition to each other. She has this influence because she is not mixed up with the strife of parties. The moment she becomes so, it is gone. Men no longer sheathe the sword in her presence. She loses her peculiar privilege as a woman—to be a reconciling bond. Besides the terrible risk of destruction to domestic peace and union, that would ensue from difference of political opinions between husbands and wives, fathers and daughters, brothers and sisters—woman's outward activity in the public sphere would only aggravate the strife of parties. Her peculiar nature exposes her to the worst influences of politics. The predominance of feeling in her constitution, makes her apt to be carried away by popular excitement, and under its impulses to become less scrupulous, more passionate and more unjust than men—a truth history has given more than one memorable proof of.

"Thus by engaging actively in politics and public life, you desert the only sphere in which you can serve your country, to enter into one where you are not needed, can do no good, and will surely work harm. You violate the great moral order of things, established in your very nature and relations; and this inevitably involves the ruin of your proper character as women, and thereby the ruin of the dearest interests of society and of the human race.

"Away from the sacred sphere of home, eagerly mixing in politics and public life, competing with the men in all careers, challenging and clutching your rights at every turn—how could you preserve the gentleness, tenderness, refinement, delicacy, reserve, purity, modesty—in a word, the chastity (by which I mean far more than is ordinarily meant) which constitutes the glory and charm of womanhood—that which all men, the rudest and coarsest respect and show their feeling of, when, in the presence of a true woman, violence and ribaldry are hushed—that which in natures of better mould and finer culture begets the sentiments of reverence and chivalric devotion—that which even the worst of men demand in their sisters and their wives? Your womanhood gone, all is gone—gone man's reverence for woman, to the great detriment of the best and noblest parts of man's nature—and gone forever from you all that draws man to you now in true manly love. Man wants a woman for his wife,

a woman in his home, and not another man. He
will not marry you, when you become what your
notions would inevitably make you. And without
marriage, the dissolution of society and the extinction of the human race is sure. The brute instinct
will suffice for brutes, but not for the continuance
of the human race, and if it could it would be the
continuance of a species not worth continuance.

"This is what would come of your notions, if
carried fully out in universal practice.

"But I have no fears. God in the heart of
womanhood has provided a security for His Divine
order of things, against such foolish and pernicious
notions. Exceptional women may adopt and spread
them all they can. Upon the great mass of women
you will produce not the slightest impression. You
may temporarily mislead a few true women. But
the first touch of honest love for a right manly man,
will put all this nonsense out of their heads. The
lovely Paulina Paul is, I think, a true woman at
heart. She is young, and a little bewildered by
your sophistries now, but the time of her awakening will come; and then, as a happy wife and
mother, I am sure she will be ashamed to remember

her orations here to-day. The St. Anthony has no vocation for love and marriage. Her case is hopeless. But the number of such is small, and never will be large. It would stand in the way of God's plans for the world if it were otherwise."

"There, Professor Clare, that is what I might have said, if I had said any thing."

"I almost wish you had said it," replied the Professor.

"I am glad he did not," said Mrs. Oldham, "though I have no fault to find with the matter of it. Yet I am scandalized by the way you put some things, and the expressions you use."

"I am sorry for that," said the Doctor, "but it can hardly be well avoided, and I trust there is nothing improper in them."

"But, Professor, I did preach the substance of this discourse in church last Sunday evening; and it happened the next day that I was giving an account of it at Pelham's, when a lady on a visit there said, with an air of surprise and grave rebuke:

"'Did you preach this on the *Sabbath?*'

"'Yes, madam,' I replied, 'on Sunday evening, and I took for my text the words of St. Paul (Ephesians v. 22): *Wives! submit yourselves unto your own husbands, as unto the Lord; for the husband is the head of the wife, even as Christ is the Head of the Church. . . Therefore as the Church is subject unto Christ, so let the wives be to their own husbands in every thing.'*

"'Well,' said she, '*Paul* says he sometimes spoke like a fool, and I think he did when he said that.'

"I smiled inwardly at the good lady's sort of reverence, which could speak thus of St. Paul, and be shocked at my desecration of the Lord's day, or *Sabbath*, as she called it; but did not tell her my thoughts. She said she had many sympathies with the Woman's Rights women. I said I perceived it, though I was not aware of it before, and could only be sorry that my text and sermon, as well as the day I took to preach it, seemed displeasing to her taste."

CHAPTER XXIII.

ON DEE-DEEING.

"I SEE, husband, that your friend, Mr. Langdon, has been made a D. D."

"Yes, poor fellow, I was writing to him a few days ago, and said in a postscript: 'So you have got the handle to your name. Are you not ashamed?' I had a letter from him this morning, in which he asks what he has to be ashamed of. I wrote immediately in reply. But the letter has not gone yet. Would you like to hear it?"

Mrs. Oldham said she would.

"It is in my drawer," said the Doctor, turning to open it.

Mrs. Oldham was at the moment putting away some things in her drawer, having drawn it fully out—pulling, of course, the Doctor's drawer under the table out of his reach.

"Ah, my drawer gone! But take your time,

my dear; you wouldn't sleep well if you left any of your knick-knacks out of place or the least awry. I can wait. A good thing this make of our drawers—a good discipline. John Wesley tells us that while he was among the Moravians, his life was so directed by rule, that if he was engaged in writing a letter when the bell struck, he was required to leave off immediately, without stopping to complete an unfinished word. The object of the rule —they told him—was to mortify the 'lust of finishing.' That is a lust that does not need any mortifying in me, or in Lilly either—unless when she gets hold of a new book of Miss Yonge's, or some other charming story. But it is a lust that is very strong in you, and perhaps I might help to a little salutary mortification of it, by insisting on your shutting your drawer the instant I want to open mine. But then I should lose the chance of exercising my own patience, and might try yours, which needs no trial, besides interfering with your bump of order, which I have a great respect for."

"Well, husband, my lust of finishing is not so strong but I can lay aside the most fascinating book, when I have any thing else to do—as I have just done with Adam Bede, in order to write a letter to my mother."

"That is true, wife, I am bound to confess, that if your lust of finishing is very strong, your sense of duty is stronger, and I should not need to interfere in any case where duty was concerned."

"I have finished now," said she, "and you can have your drawer. So let me hear your letter."

"Here it is," said the Doctor, taking it out and beginning to read :

"My Dear Langdon,

"Do you ask what you have to be ashamed of? Why, of being made a D. D., of course.

"You have fallen from an eminence. You have dropped out of the select and distinguished circle of the un-dee-deed, into the great titled herd. You have lost an honorable and enviable distinction.

"Nor this alone ; you are now under the necessity of submitting to be impaled on one or the other of the sharp horns of a piercing dilemma.

"For know, O my unhappy friend, that in regard to this matter of dee-dee-ness, or state of being dee-deed, or un-dee-deed, there are four possible predicaments. There are :

1. The deservedly, and ⎫
2. The undeservedly ⎬ un-dee-deed.
3. The deservedly, and ⎫
4. The undeservedly ⎬ dee-deed.

"Now, when you were in the un-dee-deed state—fortunate man if you had known your good fortune—no man could reasonably ask you if you were not ashamed. For you belonged either to the first or to the second class. If to the former, it was no cause of shame that you had not a title you did not deserve to have—rather the shame would have been in having it. If to the latter, it was surely no cause for shame to you, whatever it might be to the undiscerning and ill-judging colleges that neglected to adorn your just desert. And either way, whether deservedly or undeservedly un-dee-deed, nobody could, without ridiculous absurdity, ask you if you were not ashamed of being a D. D., when you were not one. One might as well ask if you are not ashamed of being a rhinoceros, when he knows, and you know, and all the world knows you are not a rhinoceros.

"Nor, for the same reasons, had you any cause to be ashamed on account of the company you were in—the honorable fraternity of the un-dee-ded; for they, like you, had no cause to blush for themselves.

So therefore there was absolutely no ground for the question.

"But now you have not only lost the simple manly dignity of an untitled name, and fallen from the select circle of the un-dee-deed, into the great and ever-increasing herd of clerical D. D.'s, likely to be augmented by a host of unclerical D. D.'s, led on by my friend, the clever and eloquent lay-preacher just decorated at Cambridge, but, as I said, you are liable to be pierced by one or the other horn of a cruel dilemma.

"For, either you are or you are not possessed of the intrinsic and essential quality of true dee-dee-ness—a profound knowledge of theology, and an aptitude to teach it, withal. If you are, you have reason to be ashamed of the great company of mere titular D. D.'s you have fallen into; and if you are not, you are yourself a mere titular D. D., and have reason to be ashamed of yourself for being a sign without the thing signified—a doctor's doorplate with no doctor within—in short, a pretence and a sham; and so, either way, you have reason for being ashamed. But I am not of the spirit of the man who, in a time of some quite wide-spread disaster, exclaimed: 'Well, wife, thank God our neighbors are as bad off as ourselves.' On the contrary, I subscribe myself,

"With hearty condolence,

"Your sympathizing friend,

"OLDHAM."

"But, husband, you don't mean that your friend Langdon is not deserving of his title?"

"No, my dear, he is an abler man, and a better theologian, than nine-tenths of those that have it. But our whole system of academic degrees is an absurd farce. The degrees in the arts are conferred in course on young men, four-fifths of whom would find it hard to stand a strict examination upon the latinity of their diplomas. And as to the honorary degrees, they are no honor at all. Popular city preachers, or ministers of important parishes, are made D. D.'s, who could not, for their lives, give a clear and accurate statement of the doctrines and logical connection of the doctrines of a single theological system, still less a just, comparative and critical exposition of the differences and agreements of the different systems, and, least of all, of the principles that underlie and determine their systematic relations; while LL. D.'s light on the surprised heads of men who know no more of Civil, or of Canon law, or of the difference between them, than Field Marshal Wellington and Marshal Blucher ell-ell-deed at Oxford, or General Jackson and General Taylor ell-ell-deed by our own University of Cambridge."

"What are these degrees worth, then, husband?"

"Nothing at all, my dear, and never will be, until they are given only when well-earned."

CHAPTER XXIV.

TWEEDLEDUM AND TWEEDLEDEE.

"Ah, my son," said the Doctor one day, talking to Phil, "get the habit of always discerning the distinct in the inseparable. There are some persons that are forever confounding them. They cannot distinguish between things that always go together, especially if they are at all blended or lie very close to each other."

"But there is another class of persons," said Phil, "that are forever puzzling a plain question, or avoiding the force of a just argument, by distinctions without a difference—mere tweedledum and tweedledee."

"Ah, Phil, rail not at the distinction between tweedledum and tweedledee—for there is a real difference between them, and often a momentous difference. Beware how you think contemptuously of it. No matter how slight it may seem, it may be of infinite consequence. The angle where two straight lines meet, may be infinitesimally small, but produce the lines and they become heaven-wide apart. It is a difference on which the dearest interests of truth and human welfare may turn. It has often convulsed the world of thought and of action. The profoundest agitations—religious and political—which history records, have sprung from it. Humanity is not thus moved for nothing. I have a great respect for the difference between tweedledum and tweedledee.

"But I have no respect for the difference between tweedledum and tweedledum; and that is a distinction some persons—I grant you, Phil—lay great stress upon, and are always parading, to the great detriment of all rational argumentation."

"They have a notion they evince superior logical acuteness," said Phil.

"Logic," said the Doctor, "is a very good thing for a good thinker, but a very bad thing for one who is not. There's Mr. Grim—he is intensely logical, but his logic only serves to illustrate the poorness of his thought. A man must be able at times to get above his logic, or below it—whichever you choose—in order to use it to any very good purpose."

"But logic is thinking, is it not?" said Phil.

"Yes," replied the Doctor, "but not all thinking. There is other thinking besides logical. There is thinking—and of the highest sort—which is the very reverse of the logical, which sees and seizes by immediate intuition, without any process of deduction, great truths, that logic never gives—all the primary principles of mathematics, metaphysics, and morals—truths that are true because they are true, and not because something else is true from which their truth flows—truths of the highest importance in themselves, and indispensable also for the uses of logic.

"Logic, my son, is of great use to those who have good sense and discretion, and know how to use it at proper times and in a proper way. But I reckon among the greatest social pests, those persons who are for having an argument on every thing that comes up, though it be a matter of fact as palpable as the nose on your face; who are not content to believe that a horse has four legs, without a syllogism running round in an edifying circle to prove it: quadrupeds have four legs; horses are quadrupeds; therefore horses have four legs; and whose arguments, even if not circular, and though their premises and conclusious may all be true, yet half the time have no more logical connection—or *hang-together-ness,* as the Germans call it—than if I should say : Adam was the first man ; Methusaleh was the oldest man ; therefore St. Paul was shipwrecked.

"You may find your familiarity with logic of great advantage at the bar, if you use it rightly, especially in a dialectical way as a critical test of the value of the arguments you oppose. But beware of using its technical forms or peculiar terms, unless they be such as usage has made generally familiar and intelligible. Show the superiority of your logical training, by the lucid order and method of your own reasoning, and by the quickness with which you detect, and the clearness with which you expose the sophistry of others—and all in the simple ordinary good English, which men of true culture find sufficient for most purposes of private or of public speech."

CHAPTER XXV.

SOME OF THE DOCTOR'S NOTIONS ABOUT CONVERSATION—HIS PRACTICE IS ANOTHER QUESTION.

"What have you been writing?" said Mrs. Oldham, one evening, as the Doctor shut his portfolio, and was putting it in his drawer.

"A slight sketch, or rather some hints for an essay," he replied.

"On what, husband?"

"On Conversation."

"Read it, will you?" said she.

The Doctor read as follows:

"There goes great tact to the keeping up of agreeable conversation, in a small social circle. The talk should be general. It is death to all quiet, rational enjoyment, to have the conversation broken up into two or three separate dialogues on different subjects, crossing and jostling each other, and filling the room with a confusion of sounds. There should be but one topic at a time, and the transitions easy and natural—the ball going round and round, so that each one that chooses, may hit it in turn, each hitting it in the right direction, to keep it going as long as it is agreeable. It is a great nuisance to have it struck wrongly—by feeble dabs, bringing it to the ground, when it should have been kept going on, or by great brute knocks, sending it off at a tangent, where nobody cares to go.

"Among the most disagreeable persons in society, is your man of inexorable facts—nothing but facts—who is always lying in wait to spring like a tiger from a jungle, or a catamount from a tree, upon any trifling and altogether immaterial inaccuracy of fact, that may happen to be referred to in passing, and pull the whole conversation to the ground, or drag it away into some thorny thicket of irrelevant debate. I have often been present where the conversation was flowing on in a full, deep, rich stream of mingled wit and wisdom, thought and argument, sense and sentiment—all aglow with the warmth of imagination and the brightness of fancy—when a slight momentary glance, in the merest passing way, at some fact true enough for all the purpose of the allusion, would bring up the inexorable fact-man, contradicting or putting right his unhappy victim, with an air as if the least want of exactitude or completeness of statement about the matter of fact, destroyed all the force of reasoning, all justness of thought, or sacredness of sentiment—though it really did not come within a hundred miles of doing so. To make a slip of the tongue, and speak of the Poor Widow's *three* mites, would spoil for him the effect of the most touching discourse on the beauty of self-sacrificing beneficence. It will not do for you to talk to him about the baseness of treachery, if you should happen to make a mistake as to the value of the thirty pieces of silver Judas Iscariot sold his Lord for; and he would instantly become insensible to the horrors of St. Bartholomew's, if you should fall into an error as to the precise day of the month on which the massacre of the Huguenots began.

"Another social pest is your inveterate punster, without the gift of knowing how to use his talent. An occasional pun, a good sparkling one, which does not disturb the current of discourse, or when there is no particular current to be disturbed, is a very pleasant thing. But who wants to have an interesting conversation wrested violently out of its course by a ruthless pun—no matter how bright and good in itself. There's Oglethorpe—he is a Philadelphian—whatever the subject or the mood of the company may be—he is perpetually letting off a volley of puns, without the least grace of discretion, some of them very poor, many of them execrable, and scarcely one of them that does not unpleasantly interfere with the course of the conversation.

"But there are few things more wasted and out of place, than the bright-minded man in the company of the dull; a genial, juiceful man, simple, cordial and kindly, playful and gleesome, full of fancy and imagination, wit, humor, fun and pathos, mingled and blended, bubbling up and running over in a bright flowing stream of grand and rich thought, noble and sweet sentiment, beautiful images, lively description, sparkling traits—all this wealth of spiritual riches thrown away upon the green, stagnant dulness of the minds and hearts around him, or worse than thrown away among swine that trample the pearls, and turn to rend the unsuspicious scatterer—envious mediocrities, imputing all to vanity, and watching for something to cavil or to sneer at; or serious 'professors of religion,' setting him down for a light-minded trifler, altogether wanting in 'vital piety'; or conventional worldly dullards, polished inanities, capable themselves of nothing but soft insipidities, or pompous platitudes, standing much upon dignity, and superciliously lifting their eyebrows, as much as to say, 'an eccentric, improper person.'

"There is another class of men, who are a great social nuisance—your formalists, of whom my Lord Bacon somewhere says something to this effect—'that it is a ridiculous thing and fit for satire, to see what shifts and contrivances these formalists have, what prospectives to make superficies, that hath only length and breadth, appear a solid, that hath also depth.' Among the absurdities of these men, the most ridiculous (if it did not also excite one's spleen) is the way some of them have of imagining they enjoy a monopoly of the gift of prophesying. Propose any scheme, advocate any plan not of their devising, forecast any results, they shake their empty heads, as if nobody's eyes were so good to see into a millstone with as theirs.

"There is something very impressive in solemn silence—to those who are impressed by it."

CHAPTER XXVI.

PRELIMINARY TO ANOTHER.

Some learned man—I forget his name—has written a history—I cannot recollect of what country, but I believe it is Iceland—in which occurs a chapter entitled " Of Owls," containing only these words : " There are no owls in Iceland."

I wish to devote a chapter to the record of a remark of the Doctor's, which I think is a negative pregnant, of more sententious fulness than even the learned historian's.

I am willing to be considered an humble imitator of the learned man, in the matter of the length of my chapter ; but I do not wish it to be thought I have borrowed the title of it from him. I should have put it at the head of my chapter if he had never written his—for it is the only title the chapter could have with any fitness. It is as much mine as though he had not used it before me.

A learned friend of mine casting his eyes over what is said above—but not, alas! until after the *casting* of the chapter—tells me that my vindication of my title for the next chapter is needless; for that the learned historian's chapter is entitled " *Of Snakes,*" and declares : " There are no Snakes in Iceland."

Now what to do ? Ὁ στερεοτυπτον στερεοτυπτον —stereotype plates are stereotyped. It is much easier to fill out the blank of this page with a confession of my mistake, than to make the needful alterations in the plate. I do so therefore.

Besides, it is possible my learned friend may be himself mistaken—in which case all that stands above should stand. Let every reader decide, if he can, on which side the error lies ; and if he cannot, let him comfort himself with the thought how little it matters—only as, doubtless, the Icelanders would rather be without snakes than without owls, let him hope that I am the one in error : so shall the charity of his spirit be a blessing to himself—which is another comfort. How much good one may get from every thing !

CHAPTER XXVII.

OF OWLS.

"Owls," said the Doctor, "can do nothing but look wise."

CHAPTER XXVIII.

THE DOCTOR SAYS SOME THINGS THAT SOUND VERY STRANGE TO MRS. GARLAND—BAD CHRISTIANS AND GOOD HEATHENS—MR. GRIM—THE NECESSITY FOR A GOOD GOD.

"OPENED Japan to Christianity, have they?" said the Doctor. "What a pity! It did not matter much when the British opened China. The people were already so bad Christianity could not make them much worse. But the Japanese were so much better and better off than they are likely to become now."

"What shocking stuff you are saying," exclaimed Mrs. Garland. She is a friend of Mrs. Oldham's, and was passing the evening at Greystones. The two ladies were sitting on the sofa at the farther end of the library, consulting about an embroidered pincushion, when Mrs. Garland's attention was arrested by the Doctor's remark to Professor Clare.

"What shocking stuff," said she. "What do you mean by it? Do you think that Christianity makes heathen nations worse?"

"I know what he means," said Mrs. Oldham, "though I wish he would not speak in such a way. He means that bad men from among us will get there first, and make the people worse before good men can make them better."

"That reminds me," said the Professor, "of a story I have heard the once famous Captain Riley used to tell. He had occasion to put his ship on the beach, on the coast of some Mohammedan country, in order to repair her bottom, and was obliged to take out his cargo and send it on shore. He applied to the nearest Cadi, or magistrate of the district, for a guard to protect his goods from theft. The Cadi told him he could have a guard if he wished; 'but,' said he, 'can you trust your own men?' 'O yes,' replied the captain. 'What do you want of a guard, then?' said the Cadi; 'there is not a Christian within a hundred miles.'"

"Well," said the Doctor, "Captain Riley's is not the best authority in the world, yet the story may be true for all that. The Moslemim have vices enough, but thieving, I believe, is not one of them, at least not of the Turks. In the bazaars of Constantinople, I am told, the merchants are not afraid to go away and leave their goods exposed, with the prices marked on them, and if a purchaser comes along, he takes what he wants, and leaves the money in its place.

"But however this may be, it is a sad thing to consider in how many cases bad Christians have carried corruption, vice and disease among less civilized people, before the better influences of genuine Christian teaching and example could get hold of them. And I am particularly sorry for the Japanese, if the accounts we have recently had of them be correct. I have seldom read such pleasing descriptions of an industrious, ingenious, contented, virtuous and happy people."

"But why do you talk of bad Christians?" said Mrs. Garland. "It seems to me bad Christians are the same thing as no Christians at all."

"I suppose, then," replied the Doctor, "you would say bad heathen are no heathen at all?"

"No, I would not say that—but it seems to me that a person cannot be a Christian unless he is good."

"Nor a heathen without being bad?" asked the Doctor.

"Well," she replied, "I suppose some may be naturally worse than others, but none of them good."

"Why not?" returned the Doctor. "The grace of God is everywhere to make all men good, who will concur with its 'godly motions,' as the Prayer Book has it. Even the heathen Seneca could say: 'A Holy Spirit dwells within us; no man is a good man without God.' That is a better doctrine than the Reverend Calvin Grim's, on the one hand, and Dr. Pelagius Blowbag's on the other. For my part I don't doubt there may be heathen who are better men than many Christians are. There may be—I thank God—very Christian heathen, as there undoubtedly are—I am sorry to say—very heathenish Christians; and certainly a good heathen is a great deal better than a bad Christian."

"But what is to make them good?" said Mrs. Garland. "They have no knowledge of the Gospel."

"The Devil has a very correct knowledge of the Gospel," replied the Doctor; "does it make him good?"

"But he is out of its pale," said she; "the Gospel is for men."

"Well, look around you, then, in our own neighborhood, and you will see a great many men nearly as bad as bad men can be. No, my dear lady," continued the Doctor, "the knowledge of the Gospel neither necessarily makes men good, nor is it an indispensable condition to their becoming so. Men may be bad with it—bad Christians, and good without it—good heathen.

"No creed of doctrines, however true and sublime, and no code of morals, however pure and noble, can make men good by their own force alone. The Gospel, if you look at it as a mere creed or code, is as ineffectual as the Vedas and Shastras, the laws of Lycurgus, or the institutes of Menu. What is the use of advising a man with broken legs to get up and walk. Set his legs, and in due time he will walk—and run, if need be. Every man knows he is not as good as he ought to be; and no man can make himself so of his own force alone. What he needs is Divine aid—a power within him working with him to help him effectually to be and to do what he ought. Does the All-Father deny this help to any of His creatures? does He give it only to those who know the wonderful story of the way in which it comes to us? God forbid. His Good Spirit is in every human heart—a power to goodness in every one—working in the reason and conscience of all men—in heathendom through the dim tradition of primitive instruction never wholly lost; in Christendom through the clearer light of the Gospel; so that 'in every nation whosoever feareth God and worketh righteousness'—tries to obey the Divine impulse, and to be good according to the light he has—'is accepted of Him.' It is impossible for us to say how much light in the head is a necessary condition to goodness in the heart. God alone knows. But this I am sure of, that 'clear views of the vital truths of the Gospel'—as our neighbor Mr. Evangelicus Finephrase calls them—are by no means so essential as he thinks they are. I have known very great theologians with very little goodness, and many men with wonderfully 'clear views of vital truths,' and a wonderfully poor sense of honor and honesty; and, on the other hand, I have known poor ignorant women, with souls full of love to God and man, who, if their salvation depended on it, could not have told the difference between grace and great coats. I have seen them meekly and bravely bearing the heavy burden of a weary life with the noblest integrity; and I have sat by their death-beds, and have gone with them down the Valley of the Shadow of

Death, as far as I could go, and I know they were filled with a Divine peace that 'passeth understanding'—not from clear views, but from God and God's love in their souls."

"But," said Mrs. Garland, "if the grace of God is all over the earth, and in every human heart, what is the necessity of sending the Gospel to the heathen?"

"I have never admitted that it was a necessity, so far as their salvation is concerned," said the Doctor, "however much it may be our duty to send it."

"But what is the use of sending it?" said she.

"Because, though not an absolute necessity, it may be a very great benefit; because, though they can, by God's grace, be good without it, they may be better with it. It supplies more favorable conditions for a higher degree of moral elevation in this life. Unenlightened goodness is good, but enlightened goodness is preferable. The light of the Gospel increases their responsibilities, but it enlarges their moral sphere. They are judged now according to the light they have; with more privileges, a higher standard."

"But," interposed Mrs. Garland, "how can the heathen be saved without faith in Christ?

The Saviour Himself said: 'he that believeth and is baptized shall be saved; but he that believeth not shall be damned.'"

"True," replied the Doctor, "but to whom did our Lord say that? Look and see," said he, handing her the New Testament, open at the place, (Mark xvi. 15, 16.)

"To the Apostles," she said, looking at the passage.

"Just before His Ascension, was it not?" he continued, "when He was bidding them 'go into all the world and preach the Gospel'?"

"So it appears," she answered.

"Did not the fearful saying of His you have quoted, relate then to those to whom the Gospel should be preached and authenticated?"

"Certainly," said she.

"And looking at it as it stands there, should you say Our Lord had any others in His mind?"

"I confess not."

"Has His saying, then, any bearing at all on the case of those who know nothing of the Gospel?"

"Well, I don't know—it would seem it has not."

"Seem!" said the Doctor, "why, ninety-nine

hundredths, probably, of the human race, for six thousand years, have died without knowing the story of God's love in sending His Son into our world; do you believe that because of their ignorance of it, God withheld from them the grace of His Good Spirit in their hearts, and so doomed their spiritual existence to be an infinite, eternal failure of its proper end?"

"It does seem dreadful to believe so," she replied.

"Well, never think for a moment you are under any obligation to believe such a monstrous thing. Besides," continued the Doctor, "the very faith that is required of those to whom the Gospel is preached, does not consist in a mere intellectual acceptance of its truth of facts and doctrines. It is a moral and practical disposition—a spirit and will of childlike submission and obedience to what one knows to be true and right—and that is a spirit which, through God's grace, may be attained by those who are untaught in the facts and doctrines of the Gospel, and so they may pass away into a higher sphere with the very essence of saving faith in their souls, ready to unfold and embrace the truth revealed to them in the clearer light of a brighter world."

"Well," said Mrs. Garland, "I never heard any thing like this before. Did you?" she added, turning to Mrs. Oldham.

"Yes, I have heard my husband say the same in substance before. But I never indulge in any speculations on such things. I am content to leave it all to the Good Lord; I have boundless trust in His wisdom and love, to make all things right in the end."

"An excellent disposition, my dear wife, especially in a woman, and a happiness for all who do not feel the necessity to speculate, and upon whom such questions never press—if only they really turn their minds away from them, and do not, through reverence for unwise instruction, attempt to hold both sides of a contradiction, and believe in things dishonorable to God and revolting to conscience. Mysteries we must believe; he that will explain all things, and believe in nothing that is not altogether explicable, must soon come to have a creed of less than one article; for all things go out into mystery —every thing explicable rests on something inexplicable—the ground of all things must be groundless. But contradictions we cannot really believe— contradictions to conscience we should not try to believe; I was going to say it does us harm to try, but that I recollect how much reason I have had to see what a blessed thing it is that wrong-headed heads and right-hearted hearts dwell in peace together in many of the most estimable persons I have ever known."

"Well," said Mrs. Garland, "you talk very differently from Mr. Grim. I heard him preach the other day from the very text I quoted to you; and he urged the sending of the Gospel to the heathen on the ground that they were all perishing for want of its light."

"Yes, I heard him," replied the Doctor, "and the whole drift of his discourse was to the effect that God would condemn the heathen to everlasting death for not believing in a Saviour they had never heard of. I could hardly resist the impulse to get up and say: 'my friends, let us before all things have a good God'—and 'common sense in religion.'

"Mr. Grim is a conscientious man, and preaches according to what he thinks true. But his representations of God would overshadow the universe to me with an infinite horror of blackness of darkness. It seems to me scarcely possible but every child and simple uncultivated person must get the impression from his preaching, that what God was for, was principally to be ever on the alert to get occasion against His creatures for their condemnation, and that practical religion and the problem of human life resolves itself into a perpetual sharp lookout against this on the part of His creatures."

"O husband, it is painful to hear you say so!" exclaimed Mrs. Oldham.

"It is nothing but the truth, my dear, and I am as sorry for that as you can be. I don't say he thinks so or feels so himself, in any clear, conscious way. But it is all along of his natural temperament and of his unhappy religious instruction, that he should in all honesty preach in a way to beget in children and simple folk the religion of servile fear rather than of filial trust and love. It must in some cases have an influence, more or less, to repress or distort the freest and happiest unfolding of the religious spirit in them; but for the most part God and God's love in their souls is so strong, that they will take but little real harm. Which is something I am heartily rejoiced to believe."

CHAPTER XXIX.

PROFESSOR CLARE GETS BACK TO JAPAN, AND THE DOCTOR IS UNDULY SEVERE UPON CANT AND THE GOSPEL OF COTTON FIELDS.

"But to come back to where we started," said Professor Clare, "you will not deny the ultimate benefits to China and Japan, that must result from opening those countries to the influences of civilization and Christianity?"

"No," replied the Doctor, "only I must remind you that if China and Japan, and the whole heathen world, were to become civilized and christianized to-morrow, as much as New York is to-day, the millennium would be very far from having arrived. The spectacle of human society would be far from satisfactory to the demands of reason or the wishes of a good heart. Still, I don't question but Divine Providence may bring good out of man's worst doings. The thing I object to is the very common habit of making God's overrulings the justification of man's evil doings—particularly in such cases as these. What right had we to send a formidable naval force into their waters, and overawe the Japanese into a treaty of commercial relations with us, to which they were averse?"

"But," said the Professor, "ought they not to come into the great family of nations, and within the sphere of international law?"

"No," replied the Doctor, "unless they choose to do so. So far, indeed, as international law consists in the principles of natural justice, they were already bound by it on the high sea, or wherever else they were brought into relations with us by their own choice, or by circumstances other than force on our part.

"But the mere conventional rules of international law are of just force only upon such nations as accede to them, because they choose to come into such relations with other nations, as make the adoption of them a matter of mutual fitness and advantage. Every individual among us is bound by the rules of justice towards his neighbor, but he is his own judge as to the degree of intimate intercourse he will maintain with him. No man has a right to block up the highway; but every man has a right to keep his own gates shut—and even if he is not neighborly and kind in the matter, you cannot make it ground of assault or violence. So with nations. If they do not choose to trade with us, we have no right to compel them to do so, still less to impose upon barbarous nations, by force or fear, treaty stipulations for our own advantage, which we might naturally expect them to break—perhaps even calculating upon their violating them—and then to make every little infraction a pretext for invasion, conquest, or new demands. Which is very much the British way of doing things.

"No, sir, neither the British in forcing open the gates of China to the opium trade, nor our government in compelling the Japanese into a commercial treaty, went upon any other law than the immoral law of the strongest; and the motive in both cases was no better than the principle—the mere greed of gain. Yet we both try to cover up from ourselves the injustice of the principle, and the meanness of the motive, by talking about 'the great family of nations,' 'international law,' 'benefit to the barbarians,' and the like.

"I have a great dislike to hypocrisy and cant taken singly; but when they go together, they inspire a tenfold aversion. A bold bad man who scorns to deny or excuse his wickedness, is a bad enough sight; but he is respectable compared with the sneaking hypocrite, who tries to cover up his wickedness and meanness by pious phrases, expecting to delude you—perhaps deluding himself—into the notion that he is a right saintly man.

"The ostrich thrusts his head into the covert of a bush, and does not know that he leaves all his hindward parts exposed to view."

"He is a very disgusting object, sir."

"This reminds me of a pamphlet put out within a year or two, purporting to be by a New York merchant—though the man, I believe, has no title to the name—but at all events evidently a person of much low-bred conceit, who writes in bad English and worse taste. The principal thing, however, to disgust one, is the attempt to sanctify a project of mean selfishness, by the cant of Christian love. The man overflows with such sweet charity for the African negroes, that he would have them captured, and forced over here from the seats where God planted them, solely to save their souls, by bringing them under the blessed influences of Gospel light and love—as many of them only, however, as can by dint of hard flogging, be made profitable in growing cotton ! Delightful to see such fervors of Christian love, such pious concern for souls! Such mercy

> . . . . is twice bless'd;
> It blesseth him that takes and him that gives!

"One would imagine such precious Christian love would have quickened him to see and to preach a sublimer height of heroic charity—hard work and hard flogging pushed to the extent of disparting soul and body as soon as possible after the negroes had imbibed enough of Gospel light and love to save their souls, so as to make room for fresh cargoes to be brought under the same soul-saving processes, to be forwarded in turn with equal dispatch to the realms of bliss—leaving their place of earthly privilege to others : and thus, on and on, until the souls of the whole dusky race shall be saved ! It would make a brisk carrying trade. The traffic of love would be profitable. Godliness would be gain. Verily such virtue would find its exceeding great reward here, and foremost mention at the Great Day: Come, ye blessed of my Father, inherit the kingdom prepared especially for you ; for I was in darkness and ye brought me to the light and love of the blessed cotton fields. Verily I say unto you, inasmuch as ye did it unto one of the least of these my brethren, ye did it unto Me."

"But what could be his motive," said Professor Clare, "a Northern man to come out in favor of the revival of this infamous traffic?"

"I don't know," replied the Doctor; "possibly he was fool enough to be the dupe of his own cant—possibly the vanity of wishing to make a sensation (if so he failed)—possibly the mean purpose of currying favor in certain quarters—possibly a desire to add the carrying trade in negroes to his other callings—possibly the mere wish to enlarge the market for bread—temporal and spiritual.

"I can honor slaveholders, such as I know there are thousands at the South—good men, trying to do their duty in the state in which God's providence and man's laws have put them, without their leave asked.

"I can even respect, at least the honest boldness of the man there, who says: 'I don't pretend to Christian love and fine sentiment; I want more negroes from Africa for my own ends—to make money by making them make cotton for me.'

"But a Northern man advocating the revival of the African Slave Trade, out of Christian love for the souls of the negroes!

"Bah!

"I am of opinion the Good Lord finds more darkness to be dispelled from his than from the darkest Congo mind, and much more to be mended in his heart, before he can be a well-saved soul."

CHAPTER XXX.

MR. STOCKJOB PILE—ALDERMAN GUBBINS—HARDHEAD BULLION—BOB SLENDER—IT TAKES SOMETHING INSIDE TO MAKE SOMETHING—WHICH IS DECLARED AT THE END OF THE CHAPTER.

"No, my dear," said the Doctor, "Mr. Stockjob Pile is not a gentleman. He is a shrewd man, who has made a large fortune by 'operations' in Wall street, and is a great man among men of his own class, and also among flunkeys and snobs of every class. He is a very rich man, but I am unhappily unable to entertain any special respect for a man who is nothing but a rich man—particularly if he challenges deference on that account from men without wealth, but infinitely his superiors in sense, intelligence, thorough breeding and culture.

"I like a man none the less for being rich, and am just as ready to cultivate his acquaintance as any other man's, if he is something more and better than a mere rich man—a man of good sense, right principles and honorable sentiments, and well-bred enough not to expect me to seek him more than he seeks me. Money is an exceedingly convenient thing for its convenient uses, and an exceedingly important thing for its better uses, in subserving the highest development of a people in right culture and true well-being. But the mere possession of it is not the only nor the highest respectability. There are some otherwise very estimable men and desirable acquaintances, who have, more or less, the weakness of thinking their riches entitle them to be sought more than they seek you—who will give you a general invitation to come and see them, when civility and propriety require them to come and see you first. With such persons—no matter, as to the rest, how clever and agreeable they may be—I make it a point the acquaintance shall go upon the footing of a perfectly reciprocal give and take. If they can do without me on that footing, I can do without them. It is not because I am exacting in my nature; with old friends, or those whom I know to be exempt from the weakness I have mentioned, I am not the least in the world disposed to stand upon the punctilio of strict social gif-gaf. But as I think there are some things better than mere money, and of indispensable importance to the commonwealth—without which indeed no people, however rich, can advance to the highest social state—so I think the dignity and worth of those interests should never be compromised by unseemly subservience to what is merely external and material—especially in a country like this, where there is a tendency to the over-estimation of the dignity of dollars, not checked or countervailed, as in England, by established ranks and other powerful social influences not based upon mere money.

"This reminds me of a passage I was reading to-day in an Academic discourse, published many years ago by Dr. Henry. Here it is. Let me read it to you:

"'Throughout the country the great majority of the people have a profound reverence for nothing but money. Public office is a partial exception. Why should it be otherwise? They see nothing else so powerful. Riches not only secure the material ends of life—its pleasures and luxuries, but they open the way to all the less material objects of man's desire—respect and observance, authority and influence.

"'In the mean time the tone of society is debased. The *luxury* of mere riches is always a vulgar luxury. It is external and devoid of good taste. It always goeth about feeling its purse. It counteth the fitness and propriety of its appointments, by the sum they cost. It calleth your attention to its glittering equipage, and saith it ought to be of the first style, for it cost the highest price. It receiveth you to its grand saloons, and wisheth you to mark its furniture. It inviteth you to its table, and biddeth you note the richness of its plate, and telleth you the price of its wines. The *fashion* of mere riches is also a vulgar fashion. The butterfly insignificance of its life is not even adorned by the graceful fluttering of its golden wings. It is quite possible to have the extravagance and frivolity of fashionable life, without the ease and grace, the charms of wit and spirit, and the elegance of mind and manners, that in other countries often adorn its real nothingness, or cover up the coarse workings of jealousy and pretension.

"' Such must always be the tendency of things, where the commercial spirit acquires an undue predominance—where the excessive and exclusive respect for money is not repressed by appropriate counterchecks. In some countries these checks to the overgrowth of the commercial spirit are sought in venerable institutions of religion and letters, in habits of respect for established rank, and above all, by throwing a considerable portion of the property into such a train of transmission, as that it becomes the appendage and ornament of something that appeals to the higher sentiments, something that is held in greater respect than mere riches, and with the possession of which are connected dignified trusts, a high education, and the culture and habit of all lofty and generous sentiments. This is unquestionably the *idea* lying at the ground of the English aristocracy in the English constitution. Hence inalienable estates, belonging not to the man, but to the dignity; where the wealth is designed to be only the means of sustaining and adorning the dignity, of fulfilling its proper trusts, and of upholding those high interests of the country, of which the possessor of the dignity is but the representative; and where habits of education, from generation to generation, are designed to teach and impress the value of many other things above mere riches, and to connect with the possession and use of them honorable sentiments, liberal culture, and the disposition to respect and promote the cultivation of high science and letters, and all the more spiritual elements of social well-being. And strong as are our prejudices in this country, it may at least be questioned, whether a fair estimate of the evils on both sides, would not show that such an aristocracy is in many respects preferable to the aristocracy of new riches, where the elements of society are in perpetual fluctuation, where the coarse pretensions of lucky speculators, and the vulgar struggles of all to get up, leave little room for the feeling of repose and respect.'

"I don't quite agree," continued Dr. Oldham, "with every expression in this passage. I think the people of this country have an inordinate respect for public office as well as for money; and it seems to me there is a greater respect for high science, art and letters, than there was twenty years ago, when this discourse was written. Still there is a great deal of truth in it.

"It is amusing, for instance, to see the working of fashionable exclusiveness in the society among us, that rests upon commercial wealth. By the yard, by the piece, by the bale, by the cargo, are distinctions of great moment in the New York world of fashion. The wives and daughters of the man that sells by the cargo, turn up their noses at the wives and daughters of the man that sells by the bale, and never even think of the wives and daughters of the lesser sellers as belonging in any way to society—though the great world of London would laugh at the distinction, and exclude them all alike, and every thing else connected with trade, except now and then in the case of a great banker, iron-master, mill-owner, or the like, who, besides being rich, had shown superior abilities, and won a distinguished position in the political world, or in some other sphere of public service.

"The lower strata in New York may, however, work up and *crop out*—as the geologists say. Alderman Gubbins has done so; or rather Mrs. Gubbins and the daughters have. Gubbins began life as a small grocer in Fulton street—his family living over his shop; but he was shrewd, frugal and lucky, and in a few years removed his business to South street, where he made an immense fortune by heavy transactions in coffee, rum, sugar, and the like.

"Gubbins is a coarse, sensual man, fond of good eating and drinking; beyond that he has a supreme contempt for every thing but money. But his wife is clever, and very ambitious for herself and for her daughters. So Gubbins has built a great house in Fifth Avenue, with no end of fine furniture and gorgeous upholstery within, and his wife has pushed her way to a place in the upper world of fashion, by giving costly entertainments to its denizens, plenty of whom will go to criticize, to dance with each other, to devour truffle pies, and drink Gubbins' unquestionable hock and champagne. Mrs. McFlimsey of Madison square may be seen there, and her daughter Flora, although Mrs. McFlimsey declares she cannot help feeling awkward when she remembers—as she well does—the shop in Fulton street. But then Mrs. Bullion goes, and Mrs. Diamond—and what is she to do?

"Hardhead Bullion—'worth his millions,' as they say on 'Change—is of a different cast from Gubbins. He values money neither for itself nor for the luxuries it buys, so far as his own enjoyment of them is concerned, but for the deference and observance it secures. He is a proud man, not unconscious of the superior respect which cultivated persons have for high intellectual faculties and achievements above mere money; and he takes pleasure in making sumptuous dinners, and inviting men eminent in art or letters along with rich men of his own kidney, bestowing exclusively upon the latter his special attention and civilities, and maintaining the conversation upon such matters as suit their intelligence and capacity of being interested, and putting the former into the false position of silence, or of following his lead, and playing second to men not so much intrinsically entitled to deference, perhaps, as the butler behind his chair. It gratifies his pride. But those who have any proper self-respect are never caught the second time; though I am ashamed to say there are always some persons of fine parts and true genius, who are content to be his satellites and dry nurses to his pride, and to that of those who estimate the worth of a man by the number of dollars he has, or is supposed to have. What a significant and humiliating token, by the way, of the vulgarizing and morally deteriorating effect of the social predominance of mere money, is such a use of that word, Worth! that good old Saxon term, framed originally to express the intrinsic dignity, the spiritual nobleness of man.

"Bob Slender is of another type. He is a vain man; and when he had built up his fortune to the height he was satisfied with, he began to cast about to acquire social distinction outside Wall street and the Board of Brokers. He had a certain conceit of his taste in matters of Art, so he built himself a handsome house, with a large library and a spacious sky-lighted picture gallery, and set up as a patron of American Art—sparing no pains to make his house an agreeable point of reunion to eminent artists, celebrated poets, and distinguished men of letters, cultivating them with much assiduity, and thereby securing a certain distinction to himself, in the way most agreeable to his vanity; and being a really good-natured fellow, with a genuine respect for the distinction which intellectual eminence confers he has succeeded in establishing quite intimate relations with nearly all good-natured men among those whose society he cultivates.

"But Stockjob Pile is a very different sort of man from either Gubbins, or Bullion, or Slender. He piques himself upon his white hands, faultless linen, well fancied neck-tie, nicely fitting gloves and boots, correct hat, well-chosen vests and other garments, jewelry and ornaments genuine and in no excess:— in short, he is the model of a well-dressed man. He speaks respectable English, but knows nothing outside the sphere of his 'operations,' except what he gets from one or two daily newspapers, from the current talk 'down town,' and from the 'up town' gossip of the society he lives in, calling itself fashionable, composed for the most part of persons of the same sort with himself, and based upon the ostentatious expenditure of money.

"But Mr. Stockjob Pile, though excessively genteel, is not a gentleman.

"I will tell you how I came to know it. I

have no acquaintance with him, though I know him by sight. I was in town the other day, and got into one of the cars running down Sixth Avenue. The old way of collecting the fare, by a conductor passing through, had just been changed, and passengers were expected, immediately on entering the car, to deposit their fivepences in a box placed at the head of the car, under a printed placard advising them of the new way, and informing them that the driver had instructions to receive from such as could not make the exact amount, any larger coin or note, and return to them the full sum in such *'change'* as would enable them to make the proper deposit in the box. Very soon after I got in, a person entered and took a seat by my side. Apparently uninformed of the change, and not noticing the placard, he paid no heed to the driver's raps on the door to remind him. I pointed his attention to the directions. He cast his eyes on them, thanked me, and made his deposit.

"Presently Mr. Stockjob Pile came in and took a seat opposite to us. He was dressed in a very distinguished but perfectly correct morning costume. He did not comply with the new directions, and sat regardless of the driver's admonitory raps. Presuming him ignorant of the change, the man at my side politely pointed his attention to the placard. Stockjob looked in the direction, then bending his eyes upon the man, said, in a supercilious tone: 'I learned to read some time ago.' 'So did I,' replied the man, 'but I was none the less obliged to this gentleman for his politeness in pointing me to that new rule. But I beg your pardon, sir.'"

"What did Mr. Pile say in reply?" asked Mrs. Oldham.

"Nothing," answered the Doctor; "but I said something to the man by my side, in an undertone, which yet, I am afraid, reached Mr. Stockjob Pile's ears. I did not look at him, but I noticed immediately a mild smile on the face of a very bright looking young lady directly opposite me."

"What was it you said?"

"*It takes something inside to make a gentleman.*"

CHAPTER XXXI.

ABOUT CASPAR TUBEROSE AND HIS WIFE—WITH OTHER THINGS TOUCHING THE CONSTITUTION OF A GENTLEMAN.

"But what is it that makes a gentleman?" asked Mrs. Oldham.

"I'll tell you first who is a gentleman. He is a man you know—that florist that has his conservatory at the upper end of Madison street."

"What, Tuberose?"

"Yes, Caspar Tuberose."

"Who comes to church every Sunday, with that grotesque little figure of a wife hanging on his arm?"

"The same. She is crazed, poor thing! Tuberose went to England some fifteen years ago or more, and returned bringing her with him. She was young, and I dare say very pretty, when he married her; and I have always fancied there must have been some touch of romance in the affair. The fright of the voyage, or some peril at sea, I am told, gave her nerves such a shock, that it unsettled her brain, and she has never been rightly herself since, though always harmless, I believe."

"What a figure she makes of herself," said Mrs. Oldham, "coming to church—her slender form arrayed in a scant, slim dress, hardly coming down to her ankles—the little belt around her waist, or rather almost up to her arms—the old-fashioned Quaker kerchief covering her bosom, and her huge overshadowing bonnet; she is the queerest sight in the world. She has two of those extraordinary bonnets—one for winter and one for summer—both in shape like coal scuttles of the largest size, very flaring, projecting forward more than six inches beyond her forehead and face, and bedizzened with many-hued ribbons—a perfect quarrel of inharmonious colors, in Madge Wildfire fashion."

"The ribbons," said the Doctor, "are, probably, a crazy addition; but as to the rest, the bonnets and the dress are of the same fashion, if not the very same articles, she wore when she first came here a new young bride; and she cannot comprehend that the fashions have changed, or perhaps the memory of the pleasure she then felt in her array, still clings so vividly to her shattered mind, that she cannot imagine any thing else so fit and so fine."

"Well, about Tuberose, husband?"

"He, you observe, is the pink of nicety and neatness. He comes to church dressed with the greatest propriety, and in the mode of the day, with a delicate little nosegay in his button-hole. His whole presence is instinct with precision and decorum, a sense of the proper and the fit. He is perfectly aware of the grotesque appearance of his wife, and of the ridicule it is fitted to provoke in the coarse or the thoughtless. He is just the man to have the keenest sensibility to the contrast between himself and her, and the spectacle they make together. Yet you see not a trace of it in his face or manner, as he goes to church with her—no false shame, no mortified vanity, no neglect or coldness to her—not a particle of mean feeling or behavior; on the contrary, he gives her his arm with as much deference as if she were the most correctly dressed duchess in his native land—more than this, with an air of protecting reverence that represses all ridicule, and commands respect for her from everybody that sees them, as he conducts her along the street, sits beside her at church, and goes with her to the chancel rail on communion Sundays.

"That little florist, I say, has that something inside which it takes to make a gentleman—the very quintessential internal quality of one, which Mr. Stockjob Pile has nothing of. Could Stockjob behave as Tuberose does in like circumstances? No, he cannot even respect such behavior.

"I declare I wish I had a sketch of Tuberose and his wife coming to church arm in arm—such as Wilkie would have made. I would give it the place of honor there, under Ary Sheffer's Christ the Consoler."

"But, husband, you don't give me your definition of a gentleman."

"It is not the easiest thing in the world to do, my dear; so many elements enter into the meaning of the term in its fullest comprehension. It takes, indeed, as I said, something inside to make a gentleman, but it takes also something outside. Over and above the essential internal qualities—principles, sentiments, impulses—there is also included in the proper idea of one, a certain degree of propriety and refinement in speech and manners. A man may have the air and manner of a gentleman without the spirit of one, like Stockjob Pile; though where the spirit is wanting, the hollow outside will seldom impose for any length of time upon a tolerably acute observer. And on the other hand, although a man cannot have the true internal spirit, but it will of course find expression outwardly in some form—not only in the matter of his speech and conduct, but also to some extent even in the manner of it—there may still be a lack of those external requisites, derived from breeding and culture, which we commonly and properly include in the idea of one who is completely a gentleman. Then, again, a person may have the true spirit of a gentleman, and also the manners of one in a degree to entitle him to the appellation, and yet he may, in various degrees, fall short of possessing those requisites, partly internal and partly acquired—the delicate deference, nice tact, simple ease, and the exquisite grace, and courtesy—which constitute the inexplicable charm of the thorough-bred and perfect gentleman in the highest idea of the term."

"But about those essential internal qualities," said Mrs. Oldham, "what do you say they are?"

"Well, nobility of soul, honor, and the courage to do right, respect for God's image in every human soul, respect for every thing intrinsically respectable, and delicacy, gentleness, and kindness of spirit.

These, I judge Tuberose to have—he is, therefore, in essence a true gentleman, though he is by no means perfect in some of the more external requisites for a finished one; yet, I dare say Stockjob Pile—who thinks *bulling, bearing, cornering* and *shaving* in Wall street, more respectable employments than flower-growing—would smile a supercilious smile to hear him called a gentleman in any way, because he has no idea of the necessity of any thing inside, but only a certain external position and a certain correct style of dress and manners.

"Honor! What a great word, in the right worthy acceptation of it! What a world of ill-understood meaning in it! With multitudes, honor is considered in the merest external way—birth, rank, office, or whatever is valued and praised by the world at large or by the set one belongs to, whatever confers reputation or distinction in the opinion of others. The desire for this sort of honor may exist without the least desire to merit what it seeks for: to gain it, is all that is cared for. This is mere ambition—and in men of great force of mind and will, may go to the extent of a passion—grasping for power, place, or whatever gives prominence and credit in the world—working, in all the exploits it prompts to, not for the cause of truth or the public good as its motive (even though it may seek to advance them), but for its own aggrandizement, and so engendering, it may be, or tempting to hatred, envy, and all vices and crimes, to compass its end.

"But true honor is not anything merely external—neither what a man is in outward position by accident of birth or fortune, nor what he outwardly acquires. No true honor attaches to the cowardly incapable descendant of the longest line of brave and able ancestors—no true nobleness to the mean souled son of a noble father; neither to him who by base acts, or by any acts and doings of his own, or by any chance of fortune, acquires a reputation he does not deserve, or a station he is unfit to fill.

"Honor is something internal as well as external. It relates to a man's own notion of what is honorable in itself—to his own sense of what is binding upon him. True honor falls within this sphere. But within it also falls a great deal that is fantastic and false.

"How many men feel no shame, for instance, in being known as seducers of female virtue, and will not scruple at the basest lying to rob a loving and confiding woman of all that makes life worth having—and yet call themselves gentlemen and men of honor, and are so held by such as have the same notions of honor as themselves. Such an one does not count his honor sullied by doing the base thing; but tell him to his face that he is a base liar, and he will think nothing but your blood can wipe out the stain! Such a man's honor falls under the same head as the proverbial honor among thieves—only it is not so respectable as the thief's sense of obligation to hold truth and good faith to his fellows. It falls even below the moral standard of Bob Acres' servant (I believe it is) in the play: 'he had no objection to lie for his master, but it hurt his conscience terribly to be found out!' It does not hurt your seducer's honor to have his lying found out, but only to have the plain true English for it spoken out!

"But how different from all this is true honor, which lies not in opinion, not in the breath of others, nor in any thing not essentially moral. Its contents are truth, sincerity, good faith, probity, magnanimity, generosity of spirit, the courage to do right, and the strict discharge of all duties. The man who takes these into the sphere of his conception of honor, and puts his honor in them—is them and acts them—he is the man of true honor, with the sense of honor of a true gentleman. He cannot lie, break faith, nor knowingly do wrong. He will not be guilty of any mean or base behavior, even when alone, with no eye to see him. He will never take credit when he does not deserve it, nor for any noble act he has not performed. Neither gold can buy, nor wild horses drag him from the path of right. The very suggestion of selling himself to a wrong, mean, base thing, 'touches his honor.' He repels it with indignant scorn. 'Sir,' said my friend Henry Reed's noble grandfather, when the British emissary sought to bribe him to the Royal cause, 'Sir, I am very poor, but your king is not rich enough to buy me.' This scorn, with which the true gentleman repels all attempts upon his honor, is sometimes called pride; but it is not properly pride—not mere self-esteem and self-importance, generally arrogant, and sometimes supercilious, which demands homage from all, would make all humble themselves and think themselves nothing in its presence. It is merely the feeling of disdain and disgust at what is base, and that erectness of spirit which must accompany the consciousness of one who feels that his honor has no price. Yet this lofty self-respect is not so much a mere opinion of his own merits, as a homage to that in which he places honor; and so the true gentleman has an equal respect for everything respectable in others. There is no jealousy, envy, or spirit of detraction in him. Modest in speaking of himself, he speaks frankly, fully, gladly in praise of others' nobleness.

"This is the honor of a true gentleman. I was pleased to light the other day upon an anecdote of the late Gouverneur Morris, who is said to have been as true a gentleman as ever breathed. When asked for his definition of a gentleman, he replied by reciting some old version (I don't know whose) of the Fifteenth Psalm:

> 'Tis he whose every thought and deed
>   By rule of virtue moves,
> Whose generous tongue disdains to speak
>   The thing his heart disproves;
>
> Who never did a slander forge
>   His neighbor's fame to wound,
> Nor hearken to a false report
>   By malice whispered round.
>
> Who vice in all its pomp and power
>   Can treat with just neglect,
> And piety, though clothed in rags,
>   Religiously respect.
>
> Who to his plighted word and truth
>   Has ever firmly stood,
> And though he promise to his loss,
>   He makes his promise good.

> Whose soul in usury disdains
> His treasures to employ;
> Whom no rewards can ever bribe
> The guiltless to destroy.

"It is said also that Jefferson copied these verses into a common-place book, he was in the habit of constantly consulting. Both Morris and Jefferson had, you see, the true notion of the honor of a gentleman, even if they did not always come up to it in their conduct—and I certainly do not mean to say they did not.

"In contrast with this, look at Falstaff—the perfect incarnation of a base soul—not the least sense of true honor. He has no notion even of any thing but mere external honor lying in the opinion of others; and he does not value this for itself, but only as the means of gratifying his low, base appetites. For this he values it, and is willing to do all mean, lying and abominable things; though when it comes to the point of facing death or damage to his filthy carcass, honor becomes 'a word'—'air'—'a mere scutcheon,' and 'he'll none of it.' Hear him on the battle-field of Shrewsbury —where he skulks about intent only on his own safety—as he comes upon the dead body of Sir Walter Blunt: 'There's honor for you; here's no vanity. . . . . . . I like not such grinning honor as Sir Walter hath: give me life; which if I can save, so; if not, honor comes unlooked for, and there's an end.' Hear him, too, after saving his life by feigning to fall dead, as he rises and stands over the body of Hotspur, just slain by Prince Henry: 'The better part of valor is discretion, by which I have saved my life. Zounds! I am afraid of this gunpowder Percy, though he be dead. How if he should counterfeit, too, and rise? By my faith, I am afraid he would prove the better counterfeit. Therefore I'll make him sure; yea, and I'll swear I killed him. Why may not he rise, as well as I? Nothing confutes me but eyes, and nobody sees me: therefore, sirrah, with a new wound in your thigh come you along with me.' And so lost to shame that he faces the Prince with his lie, though he knew the Prince believed him not.

"But besides this sense of noble honor, the true gentleman, as he respects himself, so he respects his fellow-men and God's image in them all. His impulses toward them are delicate and considerate, prompting him to gentle thoughts and kind judgments. And these sentiments show themselves in his speech, tone, and manner. No gentleman is arrogant, or supercilious toward others, especially toward his inferiors in position. Nor, on the other hand, will you ever see in him any thing of that offensive condescension, nor that peculiar tone and manner towards them, which constantly and unpleasantly makes them feel that one thinks them beneath him, and is civil or polite rather out of regard to what is due to himself, than what is due to them. This is a great touchstone of a true gentleman. In fine, no true gentleman will ever deliberately, wantonly, or needlessly, wound the feelings of others, trample on their self-respect or self-love, nor in any way discompose them, put them out of countenance, or make them ill at ease.

"What a fine portrait of a gentleman is Bulwer's Captain Roland De Caxton! Some one has given a select list of books for a gentleman's library. Now a gentleman may read much or little—he may be a man of many books, or of one. He may, or he may not be, accomplished in letters, learning, art, science. All this is incidental. Captain Roland reads nothing but his Bible and Froissart's Chronicle. But what a soul of honor! What disdain of every thing wrong, base, mean! What delicate respect and deference for others!

Do you recollect his attempt to get out of the hall-door, where the house-maid was scrubbing the stones? I must read it to you. Here it is, in the Caxton's—that best and most charming of all Bulwer's novels, as I think. It is Pisistratus tells the story:

"Entering the hall, I discovered my uncle Roland in a state of great embarrassment. The maid-servant was scrubbing the stones at the hall door; she was naturally plump, and it is astonishing how much more plump a female becomes when she is on all fours! The maid-servant then was scrubbing the stones, her face turned from the Captain, and the Captain, evidently meditating a sortie, stood ruefully gazing at the obstacle before him, and hemming aloud. Alas! the maid-servant was deaf! I stopped, curious to see how uncle Roland would extricate himself from the dilemma.

"Finding that his hems were in vain, my uncle made himself as small as he could, and glided close to the left of the wall; at that instant the maid turned round toward the right, and completely obstructed, by this manœuvre, the slight crevice through which hope had dawned on her captive. My uncle stood stock-still, and, to say the truth, he could not have stirred an inch without coming into personal contact with the rounded charms which blockaded his movements. My uncle took off his hat, and scratched his forehead in great perplexity. Presently, by a slight turn of the flanks, the opposing party, while leaving him the opportunity of return, entirely precluded all chance of egress in that quarter. My uncle retreated in haste, and now presented himself on the right wing of the enemy. He had scarcely done so, when, without looking behind her, the blockading party shoved aside the pail, that crippled the range of her operations, and so placed it that it formed a formidable barrier, which my uncle's cork leg had no chance of surmounting. Therewith Captain Roland lifted his eyes appealingly to heaven, and I heard him distinctly ejaculate—

"'Would to God she were a creature in breeches!'

"But happily at this moment the maid-servant turned her head sharply round, and seeing the Captain, rose in an instant, moved away the pail, and dropped a frightened courtesy.

"My uncle Roland touched his hat. 'I beg you a thousand pardons, my good girl,' said he; and, with a half bow, ['proper, my dear, to a military man,' said the Doctor] he slid into the open air.

"'You have a soldier's politeness, uncle,' said I, tucking my arm into Captain Roland's.

"'Tush, my boy,' said he, smiling seriously, and coloring up to the temples; 'tush; say a gentleman's! To us, sir, every woman is a lady, in right of her sex.'

"There, my dear, is not that exquisite?"

"A beautiful picture!" said Mrs. Oldham. "I wish it could be painted."

"Something of it might be expressed by form and color," replied the Doctor, "but nothing but word-picturing can tell the whole; and how charmingly Bulwer has portrayed the scene. That Captain Roland had some crotchets about birth and blood, which he carried to a degree of extravagance, but he had the complete inside of as noble a gentleman as ever drew breath.

"As to what goes to make up both the inside and outside of a thorough gentleman, I have said there are several things in the matter of tact, ease, polish—partly natural and partly of breeding—which may exist in various degrees, all the way up to the very height and accomplishment of ideal perfection.

"The politeness of the thorough-bred gentleman, may be more or less precise and formal, according to age, country, or custom, but always there is in it a sincere naturalness, which has the effect of never seeming overmuch or oppressive. To make other persons blocks or frames, on which to hang out the finery of one's own manners—as some do—is essentially a vulgar vanity. There goes two to the success of such an attempt, and a well-bred man of the world knows how to put a stop to it; though for myself, when any one tries it on me, I generally knock under with an air of pleased and edified submission.

"We include in the idea of a perfectly well-bred gentleman, a certain cosmopolitan freedom from the provincialism or cockneyism which is generated by a narrow sphere, a limited knowledge of the world, or by the influence of trade or other special callings. We look also for an easy simplicity and purity of language; though as to the rest, the thorough-bred man may talk much or little, with more or less vivacity and earnestness, and more or less gesticulation. This is matter of nation, race, or individual temperament. An Englishman, a Frenchman, and a Spaniard may differ very greatly from each other in these respects, and yet be equally thorough-bred.

"The absence of egotism, or making one's self the centre of all interest, is implied in the feeling and just taste of a true gentleman. As a general rule, the well-bred man will not talk much of himself, his own sentiments, feelings and doings—especially in general society; but not always does the abundant expression of one's own sentiments, and the ever-so-frequent use of the first person, indicate any essential egotism. In the late Chancellor —————— it was merely the frank outpouring of the exuberant fulness of a rich mind, taking the most direct and natural course. You could see he was not thinking of himself; he was so absorbed in the interest and feeling of the subject, that he was unconscious of any thing else. I never, for a moment, thought of him as an egotist; though I have often thought so of men who rarely used the first person, or spoke of themselves directly, yet the thought of themselves and the display of themselves was at the bottom of all they said, veiled, but not concealed, by the adroitest tact of a practised man of the world.

"Another thing in relation to a gentleman's

bearing and way of speaking. I have often been amused to observe, both here and in England, a foolish affectation—foolish because an affectation—of extreme quietness in speech and manner, a studied avoidance of strong or energetic expression—as if the reverse of wrong were the only right thing, or as if there were something intrinsically fine or of superior tone in never having, or in never giving full or earnest expression to, any sentiment or emotion, as admiration, or the like. 'Nice, 'pon honor,' said the English dandy, eyeing Niagara for a moment through his glass. 'Pretty good,' returned his fellow dandy, dropping his eye-glass, after an equally brief glance.

"Some dull, heavy-minded persons, but very proud withal, and conscious of being unable to shine, or display themselves to advantage in conversation, take refuge in this unimpressible apathy, as the only ground they can stand upon. They are like bears—as some one, Coleridge, I believe it is, says—that live by sucking the paws of their own self-importance. But mostly it is an affectation springing from vanity; and though some really clever persons, who might be very agreeable, are misled by it, yet more commonly it is the folly of such as cannot say any thing better than soft insipidities; and so society is the gainer by their affectation.

"The thorough gentleman understands that in the intercourse of well-bred society, all its members stand on equal footing. He is never troubled with any fear of compromising himself by speaking to the wrong person—a snobbishness very common in our American society. He is not—like Bankfield—always on the watch to *exploit* himself (as the French say) with the most distinguished persons present, carefully avoiding all others, and scantly civil to them if addressed. He may talk more and more familiarly, perhaps, with those he knows best, or finds most agreeable; but he treats all with equal respect and courtesy.

"Courtesy! That is another word of fine import, second only to honor in the idea of a thorough gentleman. No two words together, perhaps, go so nearly to express the idea. Courtesy implies something outward in manner; yet a merely formal courtesy, springing (it may be) from fastidious pride, or from polished selfishness, is held of little worth. Its hollowness is instinctively felt by every finely strung heart. It gives no pleasure and conciliates no regard, but awakens only displeasure and dislike. Genuine courtesy is that which is animated by a gentle and kindly spirit—which, as it comes from the heart, so it always goes to the heart. But, on the other hand, although a gentle spirit will prompt a gentle manner, as well as gentle thoughts and judgments towards our fellowmen, and although a kindly heart will prompt kind words and a kind voice, yet these two together do not make up what we understand by the word courtesy. True courtesy is, in its idea, the perfect outward form of the gentle and kindly spirit—the flower and aroma that springs from those twin roots. Not all gentle and kindly persons can be properly called courteous. The spirit may be there, but not the form. Where these are united, there is complete and perfect courtesy—one of the most graceful and gracious, lovely and winning things that delight human eyes, and charm human hearts."

CHAPTER XXXII.

THE DOCTOR'S HORSE—WHAT AND WHY ABOUT HIM.

THE Doctor has a saddle-horse, and takes a daily ride. But unlike Doctor Daniel Dove's immortal horse Nobs, there is nothing extraordinary in the story of the parentage and birth of Doctor Oldham's *Dick*—that is to say, nothing so far as the Doctor is aware. All that he knows about him is that he first drew the vital air on the plains of Mexico; and this is a matter of credible tradition —confirmed by Dick's looks and habits, rather than of the Doctor's own knowledge. Fred tried at first to get him registered in the family vocabulary as Richard Lionheart, but finally acceded to the designation of Richard Mustang, as having reference to his country and his race, which name Phil maliciously prolongs to "Richard Mustang Liniment," to the great disgust of Fred; and the Doctor often shortens to "Dick Musty," to Fred's scarcely less displeasure.

It may be that if Dick's story could be known, the faithful record would be as extraordinary and romantic, and as trying to the modesty of Miss Prim, as the story of Nob's parentage was to the Directresses of the Book Club that insisted on extracting the offending chapter—by a *scissorsean* operation—before Southey's book was allowed to go its village round. But Miss Prim's propriety will not be shocked by any thing I have to recount concerning Dick's father and mother, for it is not known who his parents were, and so I could not set down any thing about their behavior, in a strict historical way, but only quite generally, as matter of necessary inference. There is ample scope, indeed, in the absence of known facts—and the greater from the entire absence of them—for acute and erudite conjecture of things neither impossible nor improbable, which I might put together with such art and skill, as to make them pass for true; as many biographers supply the lack of known events in the early days of distinguished men, or as some celebrated historians illuminate a dark period in the history of the human race.

But I have a reverence for historical truth, even in the pedigree of a horse, and as I know nothing of Dick's, I say nothing. Indeed, if I knew ever so much, it would not be pertinent to my purpose to recount it; for I have introduced Dick not for his own sake, but because Dick's ways and his master's ways together, are now and then the cause of odd mishaps, one of which connected itself in the Doctor's mind with another horse, which was connected with a calamity that was connected with the greatest blessing of the Doctor's life, as he justly regards the occasion that led to his gaining the greatest earthly treasure, a good wife. But for Dick, it is quite possible I might never have learned the story of that calamity, but for which there would have been no Doctor and His Wife; and so this immortal book would never have seen the light.

There is a great deal more in things than some people think.

CHAPTER XXXIII.

ALL-HANG-TOGETHER-NESS.

THOUGHTFUL Reader! Did it ever occur to you to think the thought I would suggest by the word I have placed above? If you have ever perpended it deeply and long, I need not tell you it is something to bewilder the mind in the attempt to grasp and follow it.

What a storehouse is the mind of man! filled with images of every thing we get by our senses, and with ideas, thoughts, feelings, in the intellectual and moral sphere, and all of them, images, thoughts, feelings, married to words that more or less clearly and vividly represent and reproduce them. A storehouse of what capacity! made to contain the experiences of Eternity, where nothing once deposited is ever lost—many things gone perhaps from the present memory of the moment, but there, and may be recalled. A brain fever may quicken what has slept in the mind a long lifetime—as seen in those Pennsylvania Swedes that Rush (I believe) tells us of, praying on their death-beds, in their mother tongue, the little prayers of their childhood—prayers and a tongue gone from their recollection for threescore years or more.

The records of a whole life are rendered up to memory in a moment, in the case of drowning men —as recovered persons say.

What may not death do for us all?

It is astounding to consider the universe concentrated in the unity of a single consciousness. But for this unity of consciousness, nothing in the storehouse of the mind could be said to be truly there. Yet what an unspeakable chaos would this storehouse be, what useless lumber all its treasures, were it not for the ways by which they are connected, and through which they may be evoked.

Most curious and wonderful is it to think how all things are tied and linked together, so that there is not one single thing—object, image, thought, word—but is connected with every other thing— object, image, thought, word—in the universe, connected more or less nearly or remotely, and, it may be, in half a score of ways, by relations of cause and effect, substance and quality, universal and particular, genus and species, sameness and difference, likeness and unlikeness, nearness or distance in time or place. Just as there is not a single point in the infinitude of space from which you cannot go to every other point—if not in an actual or practical, yet in a mathematical and theoretical way ; so there is not an object for the senses, nor an image for the fancy, nor a conception, nor a thought, but will carry you (if you allow it) away over hill and dale, across plains and rivers, to the topmost peaks of the highest mountains ; across seas and oceans to the world's end ; to the planets ; to the utmost stars whose light has been travelling for ages toward our world, and has ages yet to travel before it will strike our orb ; and so onward and outward in every conceivable line of motion, through all space and through all time.

Behold a symbol, or rather the suggestion of one :

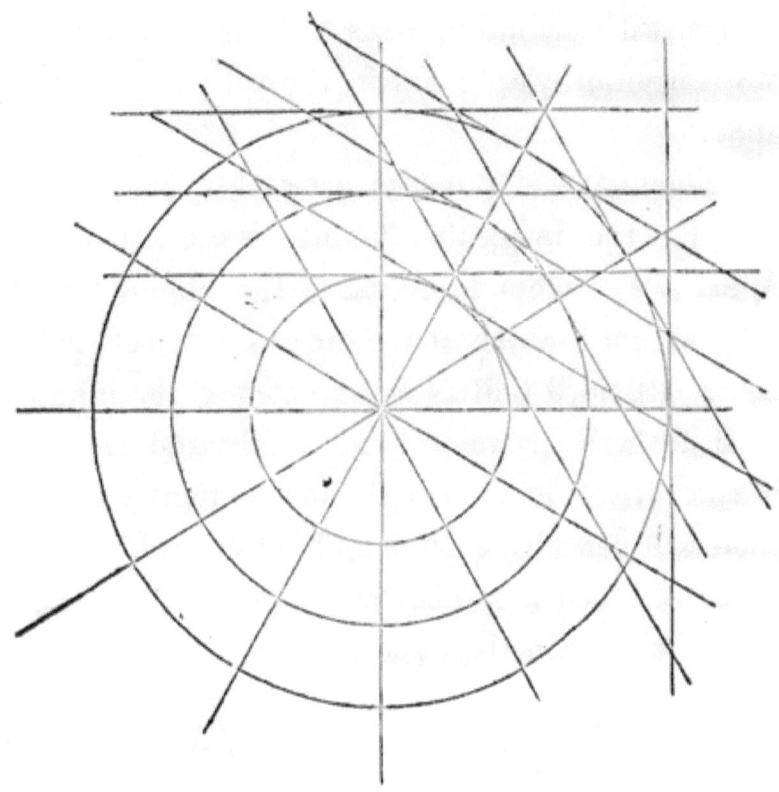

Now, thoughtful reader, consider—that this common centre may be anywhere, and consequently that every point in the infinitude of space may be the centre of such a figure lying in every plane.

Therefore try to bring clearly before thy mind's eye infinitude, in the boundless height and depth and length and breadth of its sphere and plenitude, thus diagrammed : an infinite series of concentric spheres, and every point in infinitude a centre, with radiating lines cutting and tangents starting from every point in the periphery of every sphere.

Thou canst not indeed get a clear image of all this, for the imageable infinite is a contradiction. When we attempt to measure the absolutely infinite, we get nothing at the greatest but the indefinitely extended finite—a mere zero of the infinite.

I am well aware of this : I only said try ; and if thou triest long enough and patiently enough, thou wilt conceive enough and get enough of image to be to thee a symbol of the *all-hang-togetherness* of things in the mind of man.

To me at times much revolving this matter, it becomes something quite appalling to consider what and how much may be involved in the utterance of a single word. It matters little what one. Take any one at hazard out of the dictionary, from Abaca to Zythum—if you can tell what these words mean, most courteous reader, without looking them out in the dictionary, you can tell more than I could two minutes ago—take any word out of Webster's Dictionary—and it is said there are some fourscore thousand of them; or any one out of the biographical, geographical, statistical, economical, or scientific dictionaries—amounting, for aught I know, to as many thousands, or more than as many thousands more—each of which words will stand connected, according to your knowledge, with all other words of all the other tongues you know—take any word, I say, and who can tell what a length of travel it may entail. It is frightful to consider how far from country, home, and friends, the man that utters it or hears it may be compelled to go. And so absolutely numberless are the roads that start from that single word—straight, crooked, circling, zig-zag—with myriads of crossings and re-crossings, turnings and returnings, junctions and partings, confluences and divergences—as you conceive, by considering the diagram.

Your course may take any direction of the compass.

It may take any line of progress.

I would illustrate the subject by a special diagram or two, but I should instantly remind such a reader as I take you to be, of Tristram Shandy's figure of the progress of his story, and the suggestion of that is enough for you; as for those that have not seen it, let them look and see.

Thoughtful Reader! If you have meditated upon this matter, I need not tell you it is something to make one's head ache, if one goes on long in the attempt to grasp all the possibilities of the problem.

If you have not, try it.

Take any word, and follow out your thoughts, setting down the single words, or the prominent word of any fact, scene, thought, that may be successively suggested. I will give you the beginning of an example:

    Light,
    Darkness,
    Sun,
    Stars,
    Creation,
    Moses,
    Eden,
    The Devil,
    Milton,
    Homer,
    Greece,
    Troy,
    Æneas,
    Italy,

Louis Napoleon,
The Uncle,
St. Helena,
Louis Philippe,
Ups and Downs,
Solferino,
Villafranca,
Cigarettes,
Vive la Bagatelle,
Oxenstiern,
Miss Bremer,
etc., etc., etc.

Thus you see I have been back to the beginning of things, and thence from country to country, from person to person, and from thing to thing, down to this day, and I might go on through all time—and not without reason, for every step of the way. And you will consider, too, that each word in this list might have suggested other words, and led off in innumerable other directions in other series of connections. At the word *Darkness*, for instance, it might have gone thus:

DARKNESS,
Lamps,

> Ruskin,
> Pre-Raphael,
> etc., etc.

Or thus:

> DARKNESS,
> Gas,
> Windbags,
> Stump Orators,
> Democracy,
> The Devil,
> etc., etc.

At the word *Stars* thus:

> STARS,
> Herschell,
> Cape of Good Hope,
> De Gama,
> Indies,
> Columbus,
> Americus Vespuccius,
> The way with the world,
> etc., etc.

At the word *Moses* thus :

    Moses,
    Pharaoh,
    Joseph,
    Mrs. Potiphar,
    Cream Cheese,
    Howadji,
    Nile,
    Pyramids,
    Bricks,
    Fugitives,
    Catch Law,
    Democracy,
    The Devil,
    etc., etc.

At the word *Troy* thus :
    Troy,
    Hector,
    McIntyre,
    Highlanders,
    Scythes,
    Preston Pans,
    Col. Gardiner,
    Pretender,

Flora McIvor,
Waverley,
Wizard,
Witches,
Salem,
Hawthorne,
etc., etc.

These are the merest hints in the way of solving the stupendous problem, of what may come of a word if you engage to follow it. If I had an acre of parchment, instead of these tiny pages, I could draw you something, in the fashion of the old genealogical trees, that might better show you what may spring and branch from the root and stem of a single word ; though that would be also the merest beginning of a complete exemplification. But then an acre of parchment might answer to suggest to you, O thoughtful Reader ! more than ten thousand square miles of it could contain. You would see that every word—if it have not, like every human being, two parents, four grandparents, eight great-grandparents, sixteen great-great-grandparents, and so on, in a geometrical series—has, nevertheless, numberless children, grandchildren, great-grandchildren, great-great-grandchildren, and collateral descendants, in an infinitely expanding series of more than geometrical proportion.

Besides, you must consider that the progeny of a single word, the lines of descent, the branchings and offshootings, may be as various as there are various minds. I once tried half a dozen of my friends with the word *Boots ;* and I will give you the list which each one wrote down :

I.	II.	III.
BOOTS,	BOOTS,	BOOTS,
Shoes,	Leather,	Suwarrow,
Slippers,	Calf,	Crimea,
Sandals,	Bull,	Wellington,
Washing,	Wooden shoes,	Waterloo,
Christ,	Mont Blanc,	Napoleon,
Peter,	Supper,	Guards,
Judas,	Dance,	Irish,
Arnold,	Pharisees,	Fontenoy,
Gen. Lee,	Hypocrisy,	Louis XIV.,
Geo. H. M.,	Cotton Gospel,	etc., etc.
N. Y. Hist. Soc.,	etc., etc	
etc., etc.		

IV.	V.	VI.
BOOTS,	BOOTS,	BOOTS,
English Inn,	Bootmaker,	Cobbler,
"Mine ease,"	Cobbler,	Wax,
Falstaff,	Waxend,	Twine,
Francis,	Backsides,	Roses,
"Anon, anon, sir,"	Pumps,	Bowery,
	Silk Stockings,	Rowdy,
Shakspeare,	Calves,	Lize,
Theatre,	Grenadiers,	Satan,
John Wesley,	Wellington,	Asmodeus,
Astor House,	Napoleon,	Sticks,
Fanny Kemble,	etc., etc.	Gum,
etc., etc.		Water,
		"Foam,"
		Spitzbergen,
		etc., etc.

In these lists the connection of the words in the minds of the several writers, is for the most part easy enough to be seen by the intelligent reader, although in some cases it would seem to be owing to something casual and incidental. The last list was given me by my bright-minded young friend Susan Garland, from whose clever and excellent mother I at the same time received the one that stands second above. In Susan's, there is a subtle poetic association, linking the cobbler's twine with the roses that fair fingers twine; and an equally subtle link connecting the maiden's rose-bower with the Bowery street of New York.

But enough for the thoughtful reader; to the one who does not think, more would be so much more thrown away.

"FUDGE!"

I make no doubt of it.

"I don't see what it has to do here."

Very likely not.

"But what made you bring it in here?"

The Doctor's horse.

ΦΩΝΗΣΩ ΣΥΝΕΤΟΙΣΙΝ.

CHAPTER XXXIV.

L'ENVOY, PERHAPS.—CONTAINING SOMETHING NATURAL—AND ALSO SOMETHING SUPERNATURAL, FROM WHICH NOTHING CAME EXCEPT SOME NATURAL REMARKS OF THE DOCTOR'S.

I was sitting in my study, going over in my thoughts the various sorts of good readers invoked by good authors, and setting down the names as they occurred to me:

>Courteous,
>Gentle,
>Kind,
>Candid,
>Benevolent,
>Friendly,
>Intelligent,

Discriminating,
Sagacious,
Judicious,
Learned,
Thoughtful,
Wise.

I stopped, when thus far, in a musing way, making unconsciously on the paper the Doctor's favorite cypher:

Whether the forming of the monogram acted in this case as a charm or spell, I know not—it never had any such mystic power before; but now . . . . .

Forth from the invisible vacant space
Dimly emerged, thick clustering, half seen forms,
Hovering and peeping through the airy veil,
—Ever blank vacancy to unpurg'd eyes—
And then the veil itself dissolved away,

> And dear familiar faces one by one
> Took form distinct, where form was none before,
> And smiles of pleasant recognition filled
> The peopled air a moment since so void.

In short, I was surrounded by a throng of EIDOLA, or spiritual forms of readers—a crowd of pleasant faces—not a disagreeable one among them, not a captious, or caviling, or cynical, or sneering—not a dull or incapable one, not even a critical one in the sense of one who reads merely in order to pass a judgment; but every sort of good reader ever apostrophized by good authors; and not only the specific or representative forms of the different sorts, but scores of individual images of each several sort—ten times as many as the little room could have held if they had come in proper solid bulk, and ten times ten as many, if the feminine ones had come, needing room not only for their proper bulk, but also for the vast environments of hoops or crinoline, in the midst of which they ordinarily go about. But appearing, not indeed *in puris naturalibus*—which they knew to be improper even for spirits, but very becomingly draped in the pure EIDOLON, or image way, there was plenty of space for them all, without the least jostling or crowding of hoops. Which fact persuades me it was not without reason the old schoolmen entertained the question, how many angels could be accommodated on the point of a needle, and also the question whether those celestial creatures could not go from one point in space to any other point, however remote, without going through the intermediate points. And this again reminds me, suggestively, of the truth enunciated by Mr. Shandy, when he said: "it is not without reason, brother Toby, that learned men have written dialogues upon long noses." Which reminds me again of the remark Dr. Oldham (who has a wonderfully generalizing faculty of mind) made upon Mr. Shandy's observation—namely, that all things either have a reason, or else have no reason at all; of which latter sort are all the greatest and truest truths, God, and Duty, and all Divine-Eternal things. If the remark seem to any one obscure or worse, I am sorry for him; it is not my fault. Perhaps it may be the fault of the remark. Perhaps not.

"But what of the vision? What came of it?"

Well, nothing came of it.

"Indeed! Then methinks it is a case of large promise and small performance—a grand show of a road leading nowhere."

I am very sorry; but there was no help for it.

Only you must consider how much better it is to bring up nowhere with a whole skin, than to break one's bones by tumbling over a precipice.

But I correct myself. I did not mean to say that absolutely nothing came of it, for the Doctor came of it, and that remark of the Doctor's which I have just given, which would not otherwise have come, and which alone is worth a chapter by itself —in the opinion of those who think so. Of whom I am one.

I only meant to say that the spirits of my vision said nothing. What they might have said if the Doctor had not come, neither you nor I can tell. Only I hope, if they had made me the organ or medium of their utterances, they would have given me something more sensible to set down than Judge Edmonds' spirits make him write. Lord Bacon (since the death of the pedant king who likened his great work to " the peace of God, which passeth all understanding ") has been thought by most persons to have discoursed very respectably when in the flesh. But even if he had been as foolish as his royal critic, the stuff he now talks to Judge Edmonds would make one think of the exclamation of the man in Moliere's play upon meeting the spirit (as he thought) of his friend whom he supposed to be dead: "my old friend's ghost! How ugly he looks! He never was very handsome, and death has improved him very much the wrong way!" A terribly deteriorating place for the intellect that spirit-world must be, to make such fools of men like Lord Bacon and the other famous spirits whom "the Judge" evokes.

But my spirits said nothing;—for just as they had grouped themselves into one great living bouquet of noble and beautiful countenances, with so many varieties of fine expression of mind and soul, and I was rapt in contemplation of the sight, I was startled by a touch, and looking up saw the Doctor looking over my shoulder. I had not been conscious of his entrance; but his coming broke up the concourse. The disturbed images departed like dissolving views, until nothing was left around me but "air, thin air," and the Doctor. . . .

"What a bead roll," said the Doctor, running his eyes over the list, "but after all, the readers that every author likes best, are those who like his book. In fact, as bread, according to Lord Peter's determination, includes every other nutritive substance, so such readers become courteous, gentle, kind, candid, benevolent, friendly, intelligent, discriminating, sagacious, judicious, learned, thoughtful, and wise all at once—in a word, they become in quintessential excellence every sort of good reader ever invoked. . . . . And *Dear*, withal, which is not a name of a sort, but a word of the heart, which the author addresses to his readers, with various shades of feeling indeed, according to the person and the case, but always as implying an established sympathy and liking between them.

"And as to the Courteous, which stands at the head of your list, you may remember that while it takes something more than a gentle and kind spirit to make a courteous person in the intercourse of social life, these dispositions are quite enough to make a courteous reader—which is something authors may be thankful for; it gives them a chance for a larger parish."

But how will it fare with this book?

I am apt to think it will be liked and disliked; and perhaps the liking of the likers will not be so strong as the dislike of the dislikers; yet I shall be more gratified by the liking of those that like it, than troubled by the disliking of those that dislike it. I shall be very prone to think more highly of the judgment and taste of the former than of the latter. There is a great deal of human nature in other men besides Gil Blas's Archbishop.

Be all this as it may, if it finds enough of likers, I may find more to say about the Doctor, and more of his talk to set down.

NEW PUBLICATIONS

OF

D. APPLETON AND COMPANY,

346 and 348 BROADWAY.

Any of our Publications will be sent by mail, free of postage, to any part of the United States, on receipt of price.

The Eighteen Christian Centuries. By the Rev. JAMES WHITE, author of a "History of France." With a Copious Index. From the second Edinburgh Edition. 1 vol. 12mo. 538 pages. $1 25.

    This is a striking and peculiar contribution to historical literature. It is the historical spirit of each one of the Eighteen Christian Centuries seen through the medium of a master mind. The history of each century, from the first of our era, is reviewed and generalized, grasped as a whole: its prevailing purpose or idea individualized, and its result, as a century, given to the reader. The work is singularly original, comprehensive, clear, and masterly. It will give the general reader a clearer idea of the general history of Christendom than can be obtained in many months of study, and will prove beyond question a welcome and valuable remembrancer to many especial students of history. It has been the general complaint against history itself, that it is too much a collection of mere dates, and such a complaint is the highest eulogy of this book, which dispensing with any but the largest divisions of time, except, indeed, when a date may serve to explain or illuminate some act or event, eliminates by its spirit entirely the prevailing lesson of history.

Fiji and the Fijians. By THOMAS WILLIAMS and JAMES CALVERT, late Missionaries in Fiji. Edited by GEORGE STRINGER ROWE. Illustrated with numerous colored Drawings and Wood Engravings. 1 vol. 8vo. Cloth, $2 50.

"*The story of their missionary labors and results possesses the deepest interest to all who believe in the redemption of the human race.*"—PORTLAND TRANSCRIPT.

"*This is a book of great interest and value. Its 550 pages contain such a fund of information, with regard to the Fijians and their island country, as has perhaps never before been placed between the lids of any English book.*"—HOME JOURNAL.

On the Origin of Species by Means of Natural Selection; or, THE PRESERVATION OF FAVORED RACES in the STRUGGLE FOR LIFE. By CHARLES DARWIN, M. A. 1 vol. 12mo. 432 pages. $1 25.

"*Readers of his delightful book, 'Voyage of a Naturalist,' will recognize in this new work his power as a writer, whatever may be the scientific verdict on his theories.*"—N. Y. OBSERVER.

"*The conclusions at which he aims are so startling, that they cannot fail to meet with considerable opposition. Mr. Darwin himself is far from anticipating that they will be generally received. But he has certainly a right to demand that they shall be opposed only in the same spirit of candor and moderation by which his advocacy of them is so eminently distinguished.*"—LONDON LITERARY GAZETTE.

The Path which Led a Protestant Lawyer to the CATHOLIC CHURCH. By PETER H. BURNETT. 1 vol. 8vo. 741 pages. $2 50.

"*I was once a Protestant, and I became a Catholic. The main reasons which led to the change will be found substantially stated in the work.*
* * * * * *
In the prosecution of this design, I procured all the works, on both sides, within my reach, and examined them alternately side by side. The investigation occupied all my spare time for about eighteen months. I examined carefully, prayerfully, and earnestly, until I was satisfied, beyond a doubt, that the old Church was the true, and the only true Church."—EXTRACT FROM PREFACE.

Reynard the Fox, after the Version of Goethe. By THOS. J. ARNOLD. With 60 Illustrations from the Designs of Wilhelm Von Kaulbach. 1 vol. 8vo. Cloth, gilt, $3 50; Mor., $5.

"*This excellent translation of the well-known German Poem is presented in a beautiful form, with illustrations on every page, which tell the tale as plainly as the verse does.*"—BOSTON ADVERTISER.

Great Facts; a Popular History and Description of the MOST REMARKABLE INVENTIONS during the Present Century. By FREDERICK C. BAKEWELL. 1 vol. 12mo. Illustrated. $1.

CONTENTS:—PROGRESS OF INVENTION; STEAM NAVIGATION; STEAM CARRIAGES AND RAILWAYS; THE AIR ENGINE; PHOTOGRAPHY; DISSOLVING VIEWS; THE KALEIDESCOPE; THE MAGIC DISC; THE DIORAMA; THE STEREOSCOPE; THE ELECTRIC TELEGRAPH; ELECTRO-MAGNETIC CLOCKS: ELECTRO-METALLURGY; GAS LIGHTING; THE ELECTRIC LIGHT; INSTANTANEOUS LIGHT; PAPER-MAKING MACHINERY; PRINTING MACHINES; LITHOGRAPHY; AERATED WATERS; REVOLVERS AND MINNIE RIFLES; CENTRIFUGAL PUMPS; TUBULAR BRIDGES; SELF-ACTING ENGINES.

Evenings at the Microscope; or, Researches among the MINUTER ORGANS and FORMS of ANIMAL LIFE. By PHILIP HENRY GOSSE, F. R. S. 1 vol. 12mo. 480 pages. $1 50.

"*The object of this volume is to open the path to the myriad wonders of creation that are hidden from the unassisted human eye, and most successfully does it accomplish the purpose.*"—PRES. BANNER.

Leaves from an Actor's Note Book, with Reminiscences and Chit-Chat of the Green Room and the Stage, in England and America. By GEORGE VANDENHOFF. 1 vol. 12mo. $1 00.

"*There are no reminiscences more entertaining than those of actors, and Mr. Vandenhoff, who is a fine scholar as well as a fine actor, has succeeded in presenting his in a peculiarly agreeable and attractive form.*"—NEW ORLEANS DELTA.

The History of Herodotus. A new English Version, edited with COPIOUS NOTES and APPENDICES, illustrating the History and Geography of Herodotus, from the most recent sources of information; and embodying the chief results, historical and ethnographical, which have been obtained in the progress of Cuneiform and Hieroglyphical Discovery. By GEORGE RAWLINSON, M. A., late Fellow and Tutor of Exeter College, Oxford, assisted by Col. Sir HENRY RAWLINSON, K. C. B., and Sir J. G. WILKINSON, F. R. S. 4 vols. 8vo. $10.

"*The delightful old story-teller, who has been reverently styled the father of history, has never been presented to the readers of the English language in so satisfactory a manner as in the present valuable edition. Though commenced only about seven years since, great portions of the work have been re-written, in order to incorporate, in a proper manner, the remarkable Assyrian discoveries which have shed light upon the obscurity of the past.*"—N. W. CHRIS. ADVOCATE.

Parties and their Principles : a MANUAL of POLITICAL INTELLIGENCE, Exhibiting the growth and character of National Parties, with an Appendix containing valuable, general, and statistical information. By ARTHUR HOLMES. 1 vol. 12mo. Cloth, $1.

"*No book yet published, relating to the subject, contains so much valuable information in brief space, so convenient for reference.*"—Ev'ING POST.

"*The work was one greatly needed, especially to writers and politicians, and we think the author has succeeded admirably in his undertaking.*"—LYNCHBURG VIRGINIAN.

"*As a hand-book it will doubtless be found useful by all interested in National politics, and that includes all good citizens.*"—ALBANY ARGUS.

Loss and Gain ; or, Margaret's Home. By ALICE B. HAVEN. 1 vol. 12mo. Cloth, 75 cents.

"'*Margaret*' *is just such a character as Alice Haven can create—no unnatural heroine is she, but an humble girl, striving amidst poverty, and discouragement and toil, to do right and meet the smile of Heaven.*"—GAZETTE, CHILICOTHE.

"*This story has all the grace and freshness of the earlier writings of Alice Neal, refined and purified by a pure morality and Christian sentiment.*"—MILWAUKEE SENTINEL.

Re-Statements of Christian Doctrine, in Twenty-five SERMONS. By HENRY W. BELLOWS. 1 vol. 12mo. 434 pages. $1 25.

"*His exposition of his faith is manly, eloquent, and full of earnest sincerity ; and those who differ from him in sentiment will at least agree that he speaks out honestly what seems to him to be the doctrine of the Bible.*"—PROVIDENCE JOURNAL.

"*The volume will naturally be sought for by even many out of Dr. Bellows' denomination, who are curious to know more of the opinions of a man who has been accused of tendencies in the most widely diverse directions in his theology.*"—SPRINGFIELD REPUBLICAN.

Here and There ; or, Earth and Heaven Contrasted. 1 vol. 12mo. 25 cents.

"*The idea of this little brochure is to set in contrast texts of Scripture on the same page, the first relating to 'Here,' and portraying the sorrows of our earthly pilgrimage ; and the second, 'There,' telling the joys of Heaven.*"—BUFFALO COMMERCIAL.

D. APPLETON & CO.'S PUBLICATIONS.

Martha's Hooks and Eyes. 1 vol. 18mo. 38 cents.

"*This little book overflows with pathetic sentiment, expressed in language whose quiet quaintness wins its way to the reader's heart, and both story and style combine to form a literary tit-bit of the daintiest sort.*"—BOSTON POST.

The Probable Fall in the Value of Gold. Translated from the French of MICHEL CHEVALIER. 1 vol. 8vo. $1 25.

"*The questions embraced in the theme which M. Chevalier proposed for discussion are among the most important that can engage the attention of commercial minds, for they affect the temporal welfare of every producer and consumer.*"—LOUISVILLE CHRIS'N UNION.

The Tin Trumpet: or, Heads and Tails for the Wise and WAGGISH. A New American Edition, with alterations and additions. 1 vol. 12mo. $1 25.

"*This is a book, indeed, that every Lady must have for a hand-book, and of which no diner-out can afford to deprive himself—and it is also inevitable to that ubiquitous being, 'the general reader.'*"

Memoirs of the Empress Catherine the Second of RUSSIA. Written by Herself. With a Preface, by A. HERZEN. 1 vol. 12mo. $1 00.

"*The fact that it purports to have been written by the Empress herself, invests it with decided interest at once.*"—DEMOCRAT AND AMERICAN.

"*It is a sketch of the life of a woman as noted for her talents as for her follies—not to say crimes.*"—PITTSBURG GAZETTE.

Life of James Watt. With Selections from his CORRESPONDENCE. By JAMES PATRICK MUIRHEAD. 1 vol. 12mo. $1 25.

"*Of all men, living or dead, no one has done more, probably, to extend the empire of man,—to subject brute force to his control.*"—PITTSBURG GAZETTE.

The Roman Question. By E. ABOUT. 1 vol. 12mo. 50 cts.

"*The book before us, although written by a Parisian, and privately, has the approbation of the French Government, yet is under the public displeasure of the same Government, and its printing and circulation is forbidden in France.*"—NEWARK ADVERTISER.

"*This is a 'slashing' work—replete with facts, wit, and satire.*"—RURAL NEW YORKER.

D. APPLETON & CO.'S PUBLICATIONS.

Poems. By ANNE WHITNEY. 1 vol. 12mo. 75 cents.

"*Anne Whitney's Poems are refreshing. Who is Anne Whitney?—What right has she, unknown, unheralded, to give to American literature the best volume of Poems published by any American woman in the last ten years.*"—SPRINGFIELD REPUBLICAN.

A Manual of Naval Tactics; together with a brief CRITICAL ANALYSIS of the PRINCIPAL MODERN NAVAL BATTLES. By JAMES H. WARD, Commander U. S. N. With an Appendix, being an extract from Sir Howard Douglas's Naval Warfare with Steam. 1 vol. 8vo. Cloth, $2 50.

"*Captain Ward's Manual possesses not only a professional but an historical value.*"—N. Y. HERALD.

The Manufacture of Photogenic or Hydro-Carbon OILS, from COAL and other Bituminous Substances capable of supplying Burning Fluids. By THOMAS ANTISELL, M. D. 1 vol. 8vo. $1 75.

"*The author is connected with the U. S. Patent Office, and his position there has enabled him to present to the public the record of the origin of the infant art.*"—BOSTON ADVERTISER.

A History of the Four Georges, Kings of England; containing Personal Incidents of their Lives, Public Events of their Reigns, and Biographical Notices of their Chief Ministers, Courtiers, and Favorites. By SAMUEL SMUCKER. 1 vol. 12mo. $1 25.

"*Dr. Smucker has here made a valuable contribution to historical literature, and the student of history cannot obtain a better idea of the Augustan era, properly so called, than by a perusal of the 'History of the Four Georges.'*"—AUGUSTA CHRONICLE.

Tent and Harem. Notes of an Oriental Trip. By CAROLINE PAINE. 1 vol. 12mo. $1 00.

"*This is one of the most entertaining and instructive books of travel that has fallen under our eye for many a day. The style is clear and unaffected, and much which would have escaped the notice of a man, has been put within our reach by woman's cleverness.*"—BOSTON MONTHLY MAGAZINE.

History of France, from the Earliest Times to 1858.
By the Rev. JAMES WHITE. 1 vol. 8vo. Cloth, $2.

"*A good, clear, concise History of France has long been needed, and such is the present volume.*"—COURIER AND ENQUIRER.

"*Its 600 pages contain every leading incident worth the telling, and abound in word-painting.*"—ATHENÆUM.

"*We can honestly recommend the book as being what it professes to be, an attractive popular History of France and the French people.*"—SPRINGFIELD REPUBLICAN.

"*The style is clear and sparkling, and carries one along so gracefully from fact to fact that the reader can hardly find a place where he can part company, even for a short time, with the author.*"—CHARLESTON CHRISTIAN ADVOCATE.

Morphy's Games: A selection of the Best Games
played by the distinguished champion, in Europe and America, with Analytical and Critical Notes. By J. LOWENTHAL. 1 vol. 12mo. Cloth. 473 pages. $1 25.

"*Many friends, both in Europe and America, have frequently urged me to arrange a collection of my games, which they assured me would meet with kindly reception from chess-players generally. But continued contests during the past twelve months would have precluded my concurring with so flattering a request, had it not been for the assistance rendered me by my friend Herr Lowenthal. The Copious Notes with which this volume is enriched are mainly due to his well-earned reputation, and assiduity as an analyst, and will amply repay perusal from every lover of our noble game.*"
—PAUL MORPHY.

Breakfast, Dinner, and Tea.
Viewed CLASSICALLY, POETICALLY, and PRACTICALLY. Containing numerous Dishes and Feasts of all Times and Countries, besides three hundred Modern Receipts. 1 vol. small 4to., gilt top. $1 50.

"*It is altogether the best book for a genteel housekeeper that we ever met.*"—NEW YORK OBSERVER.

"*The beau ideal of a Cook-Book.*"—PORTLAND TRANSCRIPT.

"*A more acceptable book to a young housekeeper it would be difficult to find.*"—CHICAGO RECORD.

"*We commend this book to literary cooks and persons in search of food for mind and body—particularly the body.*"—ST. LOUIS NEWS.

"*Every housekeeper who would deserve the best compliments of her guests, should own a copy.*"—CITY ITEM.

"*The receipts, which comprise Fish, Flesh, Fowl, and Fruit, are none the less practicable from the abundance of anecdotes with which they are garnished.*"—CINCINNATI GAZETTE.

D. Appleton & Co.'s Publications.

THE
NEW AMERICAN CYCLOPÆDIA.
A Popular Dictionary of General Knowledge.

EDITED BY

GEO. RIPLEY and C. A. DANA,

ASSISTED BY A NUMEROUS BUT SELECT CORPS OF WRITERS.

The design of THE NEW AMERICAN CYCLOPÆDIA is to furnish the great body of intelligent readers in this country with a popular Dictionary of General Knowledge.

THE NEW AMERICAN CYCLOPÆDIA is not founded on any European model; in its plan and elaboration it is strictly original, and strictly American. Many of the writers employed on the work have enriched it with their personal researches, observations and discoveries; and every article has been written, or re-written, expressly for its pages.

It is intended that the work shall bear such a character of practical utility as to make it indispensable to every American library.

Throughout its successive volumes THE NEW AMERICAN CYCLOPÆDIA will present a fund of accurate and copious information on SCIENCE, ART, AGRICULTURE, COMMERCE, MANUFACTURES, LAW, MEDICINE, LITERATURE, PHILOSOPHY, MATHEMATICS, ASTRONOMY, HISTORY, BIOGRAPHY, GEOGRAPHY, RELIGION, POLITICS, TRAVELS, CHEMISTRY, MECHANICS, INVENTIONS, and TRADES.

Abstaining from all doctrinal discussions, from all sectional and sectarian arguments, it will maintain the position of absolute impartiality on the great controverted questions which have divided opinions in every age.

PRICE.

This work is published exclusively by subscription, in fifteen large octavo volumes, each containing 750 two-column pages. Vols. I. to VIII. are now ready. Price per volume, cloth, $3; library style, leather, $3 50; half morocco, $4; half Russia, extra, $4 50.

HOW TO OBTAIN THE CYCLOPÆDIA.

1. By applying to the nearest regularly-constituted agent in a city or town.
2. By remitting to the publishers the amount for one volume or more. Immediately upon receipt of the money, the book will be sent by mail, *postage paid* in strong wrappers, to any address, within 3,000 miles, in the United States.

IMPORTANT NOTICE.

Any one procuring four subscribers to the Cyclopædia, and sending the amount, $3 per volume, to the publishers, will be entitled to a copy of the work *gratis*, to be sent at the remitter's expense for carriage, or if ten subscribers are obtained, eleven copies will be sent at our expense, for carriage.

** Agents wanted in almost all sections of the United States. Liberal terms and exclusive territory given.

NEW PUBLICATIONS AND NEW EDITIONS

PUBLISHED BY

D. APPLETON AND COMPANY,

346 and 348 Broadway.

The Foster Brothers: Being the HISTORY of the SCHOOL and COLLEGE LIFE of TWO YOUNG MEN. 1 vol. 12mo. $1.

"*As fresh as the morning........It abounds in fun, and in relish of the activities, competitions, and sports of boyish and adolescent life.*"—DAILY NEWS.

"*Full of life, and fun, and vigor......These sketches of school and college life are among the happiest of their kind. Particularly well written is the account of life at Cambridge.*"—EXAMINER.

Passages from the Autobiography of SIDNEY, LADY MORGAN. 1 vol. 12mo. $1.

"*This volume brims with sense, cleverness, and humor. A lively and entertaining collection of great men's thought and quick woman's observation; a book to be read now for amusement, and to be sought hereafter for reference.*"—LONDON ATHENÆUM.

"*A charming book. It is long since the reading public has been admitted to so great a treat as this fascinating collection of wit, anecdote and gossip. It is a delightful reminiscence of a brilliant past, told by one of the best wits still extant.*"—LONDON DAILY NEWS.

Onward; or, The Mountain Clamberers. A Tale of Progress. By JANE ANNE WINSCOM. 1 vol. 12mo. 75 cents.

CONTENTS.—LOOKING UPWARDS; COLIN AND JEANIE; THE FAMILY AT ALLEYNE; OFF! OFF! AND AWAY; ENDEAVORING; EDWARD ARNOLD; POOR, YET NOBLE; LITTLE HARRY; POOR JAMIE CLARK; FIELDS WHITE UNTO THE HARVEST; THE SAND HUTS; THE DRUNKARD'S COTTAGE; THE INFANT'S MINISTRY; STAND STILL; OLD MOSES AND LITTLE ADAH; THE ROCKY GLEN; SALOME; WIDOW M'LEOD; STAFFA AND IONA; CLOUDS AND SUNSHINE; FAITH'S CONFLICT; FAITH'S VICTORY; REUNION; SUMMER DAYS; THE FADING FLOWER; THE UNEXPECTED ARRIVAL; A WEDDING DAY; THE MOUNTAIN-TOPS APPEARING; HASTENING ON; THE SIRE'S BIRTHDAY; THE SUMMIT GAINED.

D. APPLETON & CO.'S PUBLICATIONS

Shakers: Compendium of the Origin, History, Principles, Rules and Regulations, Government and Doctrines of the United Society of Believers in Christ's Second Appearing, with Biographies of Ann Lee, William Lee, Jas. Whittaker, J. Hocknett, J. Mescham, and Lucy Wright. By F. W. EVANS. 1 vol. 12mo. 75 cents.

Cyclopædia of Wit and Humor, Comprising a Unique Collection of Complete Articles, and specimens of Written Humor from Celebrated Humorists of America, England, Ireland and Scotland. Illustrated with upwards of 600 Characteristic Original Designs, and 24 Portraits, from Steel Plates. Edited by WILLIAM E. BURTON, the Celebrated Comedian. Two vols., 8vo., cloth, $7. sheep, $8; half mor., $9; half calf, $10.

"*As this task is a labor of love to Mr. Burton, we are sure of its being well performed.*"—NEW YORK TIMES.

"*The editor has raked many old pieces out of the dust, while he has drawn freely from the great masters of humor in modern times.*"—N. Y. TRIBUNE.

"*We do not see how any lover of humorous literature can help buying it.*" PHILA. PENNSYLVANIAN.

"*Mr. Burton is the very man to prepare this Cyclopædia of Fun.*"—LOUIS. JOURNAL.

"*We do not know how any family fond of the ludicrous can afford to dispense with this feast of fun and humor.*"—NEW BEDFORD MERCURY.

From New York to Delhi. By the way of RIO DE JANEIRO, AUSTRALIA AND CHINA. By ROBERT B. MINTURN, JR. 1 vol. 12mo. With a Map. $1 25.

"*Mr. Minturn's volume is very different from an ordinary sketch of travel over a well-beaten road. He writes with singular condensation. His power of observation is of that intuitive strength which catches at a glance the salient and distinctive points of every thing he sees. He has shown rare cleverness, too, in mingling throughout the work, agreeably and unobtrusively, so much of the history of India, and yet without ever suffering it to clog the narrative.*"—CHURCHMAN.

"*This book shows how much can be accomplished by a wide-awake, thoughtful man in a six months' tour. The literary execution of Mr. Minturn's book is of a high order, and, altogether, we consider it a timely and important contribution to our stock of meritorious works.*"—BOSTON JOURNAL.

Le Cabinet des Fées; or, Recreative Readings. Arranged for the Express Use of Students in French. By GEORGE S. GERARD, A. M., Prof. of French and Literature. 1 vol. 12mo. $1

"*After an experience of many years in teaching, we are convinced that such works as the Adventures of Telemachus and the History of Charles XII., despite their incontestable beauty of style and richness of material, are too difficult for beginners, even of mature age. Such works, too, consisting of a continuous narrative, present to most students the discouraging prospect of a formidable undertaking, which they fear will never be completed.*"—EXTRACT FROM PREFACE.